FOUNDATIONS

PETER ANDERSON

All profits from this book will be directed to support the work of the Go Global family, focused on discipleship and church planting initiatives worldwide. The Go Global family consists of 1,100 churches with around 75,000 members across 17 countries. To support or learn more please visit us at www.goglobalfamily.org

INTRODUCTION

Jesus said: "Therefore everyone who hears these words of mine and puts them into practice is like a wise man who built his house on the rock. The rain came down, the streams rose, and the winds blew and beat against that house; yet it did not fall, because it had its foundation on the rock. But everyone who hears these words of mine and does not put them into practice is like a foolish man who built his house on sand. The rain came down, the streams rose, and the winds blew and beat against that house, and it fell with a great crash." (Matthew 7:24-27, NIV)

Welcome to Foundations, a series of studies designed to help establish followers of Jesus and churches on biblical foundations.

Every house needs a good foundation in order for it to last. So also every life, and indeed every church, needs to be built on solid principles. Foundations, though unseen, are essential as they determine the strength and the potential of the building. Today people build their lives on many things, some build on the shifting sands of popular opinion, others build on a philosophy of life, while others base important decisions on their feelings. Jesus, however, declared that God's word is the only safe and solid foundation that can stand in the storms of life.

Merely learning about biblical truth isn't the goal of this study. The aim is to help our lives to be built on and brought in line with these truths. It is not enough to know what God's word says, we need to put it into practice in our lives and churches. Indeed Jesus said that the wise person is the one "who hears these words of mine and puts them into practice." Jesus is not looking for fans, He's calling us to be followers, that's what the word disciple means. Truly, information is nothing without its application. So if you are ready to allow God's word to inspire, challenge and change your life, then this course is for you.

Welcome to the adventure!

CONTENTS

STUDY 1
GOD AND HIS WORD

The Bible opens with: "In the beginning God ..." (Genesis 1:1)

Here we are introduced to God, the One who has no beginning and has no end. He is the uncreated Creator and sustainer of all things. The Bible does not try to argue a case for God's existence, it simply assumes as fact that He is. Scripture goes on to state that His existence and nature are self-evident truths known by all, even if many have talked themselves out of this reality:

> "... since what may be known about God is plain to them, because God has made it plain to them. For since the creation of the world God's invisible qualities - his eternal power and divine nature - have been clearly seen, being understood from what has been made, so that people are without excuse. For although they knew God, they neither glorified him as God nor gave thanks to him ... They exchanged the truth about God for a lie, and worshiped and served created things rather than the Creator - who is forever praised." (Romans 1:19-25, NIV)

God is distinct from His creation, yet we can see His glory in everything He has made from the smallest atom to the universe itself. Creation inspires worship and points to God; indeed, we exist to worship and know God. To be a worshipper of God is not odd or awkward. A life of wholehearted devotion and passion for God is the most naturally human thing to do.

> "God is not the sort of thing one can be moderately interested in. After all, if God does not exist, there is no reason to be interested in God at all. On the other hand, if God does exist, then this is of paramount interest, and our ultimate concern ought to be how to be properly related to this being upon whom we depend moment by moment for our very existence." (C.S. Lewis)

We would wholeheartedly agree with the Westminster Shorter Catechism: "What is the chief end of man? Man's chief end is to glorify God, and to enjoy Him forever."

THE TRINITY

Having established God's existence, Genesis Chapter 1 starts to unveil His true nature.

"Then God said, 'Let Us make man in Our image, according to Our likeness ...'" (Genesis 1:26, NASB)

In the original Hebrew language of the Old Testament God refers to Himself in the plural (see also: Isaiah 6:8). This is our introduction to the doctrine of the Trinity.

Christianity is a monotheistic religion, as is Judaism and Islam, which means we believe in one God. This is as opposed to polytheistic religions, like Hinduism, which believe in many deities. However, Christians are Trinitarian monotheists, which means we believe in one God who has eternally existed in three Persons.

While the word "Trinity" is not specifically used in scripture, the truth of the Trinity is clearly seen, being progressively revealed throughout the Bible. Indeed, all the main branches of historical Christianity - Roman Catholic, Eastern Orthodox and Protestant - all agree on the doctrine of the Trinity. Cults and sects - such as Jehovah Witnesses and the Mormons - would typically deviate from our beliefs on this point.

In the New Testament, we are given the names of the three Persons. At the end of Matthew's Gospel Jesus laid out our commission:

"Go therefore and make disciples of all the nations, baptising them in the name of the Father and the Son and the Holy Spirit ..." (Matthew 28:19, NASB)

It would be strange if Jesus had said: "... in the name of the Father and the Son and the angel Gabriel ...". By putting them in the same list He is giving them equal standing – all three are fully God (see also Paul's benediction in 2 Corinthians 13:14).

Here are three statements that sum up the doctrine of the Trinity:

- God eternally exists as three Persons (Father, Son and Holy Spirit)
- Each Person is fully God
- There is one God

At the deepest level the doctrine of the Trinity reveals something profound about God and about us as those created in His image: God and people are wired for relationship!

Jesus' famous prayer reveals that God has eternally existed in a state of relationship. He prays to the Father: "... you loved me before the creation of the world." (John 17:24, NIV).

We know that love cannot be experienced alone. For love to *be* love, there needs to be someone *to* love. C.S. Lewis insightfully points this out: "If God was a single person, then before the world was made, he was not love." If God was a single person, then He was a lonely God and needed to create other beings in order to experience love and relationship. In religions like Islam, God is known for His absolute power and morality. Only in Christianity is God known primarily for love, as the apostle John declares "God is love" (1 John 4:8). He always has been and always will be love.

If it is the case that God did not create us because He was lonely and needy, then we can conclude that He brought us into being in order to share with us His love and draw us into relationship with Him.

THE INCARNATION

Just as Genesis opens with a profound statement about God, John starts his Gospel with a bold declaration about the divinity of Jesus:

> "In the beginning was the Word, and the Word was with God, and the Word was God. He was with God in the beginning. Through him all things were made; without him nothing was made that has been made ... The Word became flesh and made his dwelling among us." (John 1:1-3, 14, NIV)

Religion is concerned with people trying to make their way to God. In contrast, Christianity uniquely claims that God made His way to us! God became a man. This truth is called the Incarnation. The word comes from the Latin words 'in' and 'carne', which mean 'into' and 'flesh' respectively. It means that God became flesh and made his dwelling among us.

God became a man. The eternal entered time. The invisible became visible. Jesus was never not God, but 2000 years ago He became a man. He that made man, was made man. Fully man and fully God.

> "... in Christ all the fullness of the Deity lives in bodily form ..." (Colossians 2:9, NIV)

Astronaut Hale Irwin, having returned from the moon's surface, said:

> "The most significant achievement of our age is not that man stood on the moon but rather that God in Christ stood upon this earth."

Why did God become a man? Here are some of the primary reasons. He became a man in order:

- to reveal the Father to us (John 14:9)
- to understand our humanity (Hebrews 4:15)
- to be the ultimate King (Micah 5:2, Isaiah 9:6-7)
- to die on our behalf (Hebrews 2:9)

Jesus came to make our relationship with God possible through His atoning death and resurrection.

So far in our study, we have learned that God has revealed Himself through His creation – this is called general revelation. We have also seen how He revealed Himself to the world through Jesus – this is called special revelation. But God has given the world another special revelation of Himself in the form of His written word, the Bible.

GOD'S WORD - THE BIBLE

"All Scripture is inspired by God ..." (2 Timothy 3:16, NASB)

The Bible is the most despised book, the most derided book, the most denied, the most disputed, the most dissected, the most debated, the most outlawed, the most destroyed, and the most banned book in history. Yet despite this, it is still the most read book in the world, the most published, the most translated, and the best-selling book of all time. Indeed, the Bible has inspired more music, art and architecture than any other book. One-third of the paintings in the National Gallery in London are based on biblical themes.

The French philosopher and atheist Voltaire predicted: "Another century and there will not be a Bible on earth!". Yet just 50 years after he died in 1779, the German Bible Society had moved into Voltaire's house and used his printing press to produce and distribute thousands of Bibles!

Here are some facts about the Bible:

- It was written across 1500 years and more than 40 generations.

- It was written by more than 40 different authors from many walks of life, including kings, peasants, philosophers, fishermen, poets, statesmen and scholars.
- It was written in different places, such as wildernesses, dungeons and palaces.
- It was written on three continents: Asia, Africa and Europe.
- It was written in three languages: Hebrew, Aramaic and Greek.
- It was written in a variety of literary genres, including poetry, letters, songs, history and statistics.
- It contains 3,268 verses of fulfilled prophecy.
- Every year between 200 and 500 million Bibles are published.
- It is available in more than 3000 languages.
- "The Bible is the best-selling book of the year, every year!" (Source: The New Yorker magazine).

Here is what people have said about the Bible:

"You Christians look after a document containing enough dynamite to blow all civilisation to pieces, turn the world upside down and bring peace to a battle-torn planet." (Mahatma Gandhi, Indian leader)

"Within the covers of one single book, the Bible, are all the answers to all the problems that face us today – if only we would read and believe." (Ronald Reagan, former U.S. President)

"The Bible is no mere book, but a Living Creature, with a power that conquers all that oppose it." (Napoleon, Emperor of France)

"The New Testament is the very best book that was or ever will be known in the world." (Charles Dickens, British author)

The word 'Bible' means 'a library' and as such it is not just a book – it is a collection of 66 books. Here is how it is structured:

OLD TESTAMENT (39 BOOKS)

Genesis
Exodus
Leviticus
Numbers
Deuteronomy

The Law (or the Pentateuch)

These first five books of the Bible were written by Moses.

Joshua
Judges
Ruth
1 Samuel
2 Samuel
1 Kings
2 Kings
1 Chronicles
2 Chronicles
Ezra
Nehemiah
Esther

History books

These books describe the history of Israel from the entry into the land of Canaan under Joshua's leadership.

Job
Psalms
Proverbs
Ecclesiastes
Song of Solomon
(or Song of Songs)

Wisdom books (or Poetry Books)

Job is the oldest book in the Bible. It is believed that he lived at the same time as Abraham.

Isaiah
Jeremiah
Lamentations
Ezekiel
Daniel

Major Prophets

The title 'Major Prophet' does not mean that they spoke more important things than the Minor Prophets. They are simply bigger books.

Hosea	**Minor Prophets**
Joel	
Amos	
Obadiah	
Jonah	
Micah	
Nahum	
Habakkuk	
Zephaniah	
Haggai	
Zechariah	
Malachi	

NEW TESTAMENT (27 BOOKS)

Matthew	**The Gospels**
Mark	Matthew, Mark and John were disciples of Jesus and
Luke	witnessed His life, death and resurrection. Luke was
John	a doctor and set out to investigate and record the
	events of Jesus' life. He starts his Gospel: "I myself
	have carefully investigated everything from the
	beginning, I too decided to write an orderly
	account..." (Luke 1:3).
	Matthew, Mark and Luke are called the Synoptic
	Gospels, as they cover similar material.
Acts	**History books**
	Acts chronicles the exciting first 30 years of the early
	church from its birth at Pentecost.

Romans
1 Corinthians
2 Corinthians
Galatians
Ephesians
Philippians
Colossians
1 Thessalonians
2 Thessalonians
1 Timothy
2 Timothy
Titus
Philemon
Hebrews
James
1 Peter
2 Peter
1 John
2 John
3 John
Jude

Letters (or Epistles)

This collection of letters written to churches or individuals provides us with deep insight into what God has done for us in Christ and an understanding of how believers are to live in the light of their new life with God.

Revelation

Prophecy

The New Testament ends, just as the Old Testament does, with a prophetic book.

The book of Revelation was written to seven churches in Asia Minor, but its message has been relevant to believers and churches across the past 2000 years.

While the book describes future events and the return of Christ, it also speaks into our world's current situation.

HOW DO WE KNOW THE BIBLE IS GOD'S WORD?

The Bible is endorsed as God's word both internally – in its writings – and externally – by the early church.

INTERNAL ENDORSEMENT

Moses, who wrote the first five books of the Old Testament, revealed that the books he was writing were the word of God.

> "... the Lord said to Moses, "Write down these words ...""" (Exodus 34:27, NIV)

> "At the Lord's direction, Moses kept a written record of their progress." (Numbers 33:2, NLT)

It is interesting to note that it was God's idea for the word of God to be recorded in written form. It is also interesting to consider that the very first time scripture was written down, God did it, in writing the ten commandments on tablets of stone.

Jesus referred to the Old Testament as the word of God.

> "... you invalidated the word of God for the sake of your tradition." (Matthew 15:6, NASB)

In reference to a throw away comment in Psalm 82 Jesus said, "Scripture cannot be broken ..." (John 10:35)

He spoke of Old Testament events as true historical incidents, including many which modern people consider fables or merely moral stories.

He spoke of Adam and Eve as literal people, and the judgement of Sodom and Gomorrah, the flood of Noah's time and the account of the great fish that swallowed the prophet Jonah as historical facts.

Jesus referred to His own words as scripture. He declared:

> "Heaven and earth will pass away, but My words will not pass away." (Matthew 24:35, NASB)

This clearly links to Isaiah's declaration:

"The grass withers and the flowers fall, but the word of our God endures forever." (Isaiah 40:8, NIV)

And again, in the book of Hebrews, we read:

"In the past God spoke to our ancestors through the prophets at many times and in various ways, but in these last days he has spoken to us by his Son ..." (Hebrews 1:1, NIV)

In writing this the author of Hebrews places Jesus alongside the Old Testament prophets as one who speaks the very word of God.

Paul writing to Timothy refers to the Old Testament writings as scripture:

"... from childhood you have known the sacred writings which are able to give you the wisdom that leads to salvation through faith which is in Christ Jesus." (2 Timothy 3:15, NASB)

Jesus endorses the apostles as people who would be enabled by the Spirit to write scripture:

"... the Holy Spirit, whom the Father will send in my name, will teach you all things and will remind you of everything I have said to you." (John 14:26, NIV)

Paul endorses the Gospels, calling it scripture. He writes:

"... Scripture says, 'Do not muzzle an ox while it is treading out the grain,' and 'The worker deserves his wages.'" (1 Timothy 5:18 NIV)

"Do not muzzle" is quoted from Deuteronomy and "the worker deserves his wages" is a quote from Luke's Gospel (10:7). In doing so Paul is affirming that Luke's writing is scripture.

The apostle Peter endorses Paul as a writer of scripture:

"... our dear brother Paul also wrote you with the wisdom that God gave him. He writes the same way in all his letters, speaking in them of these matters. His letters contain some things that are hard to understand, which ignorant and unstable people distort, as they do the other Scriptures, to their own destruction." (2 Peter 3:15-16, NIV)

EXTERNAL ENDORSEMENT - THE COUNCILS AND SYNODS

For the first 400 years of the church, there were many councils, which met to discuss amongst other things which books should be included in the Bible. In 397AD at the Third Council of Carthage, the 27 books we know as the New Testament were decisively agreed upon.

The question is, how do we know the right 27 books got into the New Testament, considering that there were an additional 2000 other books in circulation? Of the other 2000 books, only two books - The Shepherd of Hermas and 1st Clement - were ever given serious consideration for inclusion. Both were great books and theologically sound. They were omitted because the authors themselves indicate the clear difference between their authority in writing and the authority of the apostles. In doing so they disqualified themselves. The other book considered for inclusion was the Didache. The Didache gives us a glimpse into life in the early church and functioned as a sort of manual for believers. However, in some areas of teaching it contradicted the rest of the New Testament, and was of unknown authorship. The other 1997 books were never considered as they were Gnostic frauds - and everyone knew it.

There were three criteria that the Council used to ratify the 27 books as scripture.

For inclusion in the New Testament the books had to be written or endorsed by an apostle

- Matthew was an apostle
- Mark was Peter's secretary and as such recorded Peter's account of Jesus' life. As R. C. Sproul said: "The Gospel of Mark was really Peter's Gospel, if you will."
- Luke was a close associate of the apostle Paul

- John was an apostle
- Paul was an apostle
- What about the book of Hebrews? We do not know who the author was, but at the end, it refers to: "our brother Timothy" (Hebrews 13:23). This tells us that the author was closely associated with Timothy and therefore Paul
- James was Jesus' brother and an apostle (see Galatians 1:19)
- Peter was an apostle
- Jude was brother of Jesus (and James)

For inclusion in the New Testament the books had to be universally recognised within the church

The early church already recognised the New Testament books as scripture on par with Old Testament books.

For example, by the end of the 1st Century AD Clement (the bishop of Rome) writes to Corinth and quotes from Paul's letter as scripture. Another church leader, Justin Martyr quotes the Gospels as scripture.

As John Barton says in his book 'How the Bible came to be': "The core of the New Testament was accepted so early that subsequent rulings (i.e., the Councils) do no more than recognise the obvious."

In other words, the church did not create the canon – the final collection of books – it merely recognised it.

> "The Church no more gave us the New Testament canon than Isaac Newton gave us the force of gravity." (J. I. Packer)

For inclusion in the New Testament the books had to be in line with the gospel that was clearly understood

Whenever something true exists, there is often a counterfeit. Paul wrote that the churches in Galatia "... are turning to a different gospel - which is really no gospel at all." (Galatians 1:6-7, NIV). In the early church there were heretics preaching these "different gospels" both in verbal and written forms. The Councils only included books that aligned with the gospel preached by Jesus and the apostles.

INSPIRATION, INFALLIBILITY AND INERRANCY

Having looked at the credibility of the Bible we now come back to 2 Timothy 3:16: "All Scripture is inspired by God ..." We believe the Bible, this collection of books, was written by men but ultimately authored by God Himself. We do not believe God did this by 'possessing' the writers, who then automatically started writing. Instead, He oversaw the process, moving, guiding, inspiring and speaking through the human authors, whose personalities can be clearly seen in their words.

> "... no prophecy of Scripture is a matter of one's own interpretation, for no prophecy was ever made by an act of human will, but men moved by the Holy Spirit spoke from God." (2 Peter 1:20-21, NASB)

Some were recording historical events, for example, the Gospels.

Some wrote down prophetic pictures or words, for example, Isaiah.

Some got a revelation of past events, for example, Moses' writing of Genesis.

Some got a revelation of future events, for example, John in Revelation and Daniel.

Some wrote God-inspired wisdom, poems and songs, for example, David and Solomon.

We hold a high view of scripture. We believe the Bible is **inspired** by God, and therefore is **infallible** – incapable of error, as God can not lie – and therefore it is **inerrant** – without error.

As a church, we seek to build on the foundation of scripture. We encourage you to build your life, your relationships, your decisions and your ambitions on the wisdom of God that is found in scripture.

A life or a church built on biblical foundations can expect to see biblical results. Biblical roots will result in biblical fruits.

Just as a builder constructing a wall would use a plumb line to measure how true, or perfectly vertical, the new wall is, so too do we see the Bible as our plumb line against which we align our lives and our church.

APPLICATION

In this study, we have looked at God and His word. These truths have the potential to completely transform our lives as long as we never forget:

- It is not enough to know about God, we must know Him
- It is not enough to read the Bible, we must meet Jesus in the Bible

Jesus challenged the devoutly religious people of His time. He said to them:

> "You examine the Scriptures because you think that in them you have eternal life; and it is those very Scriptures that testify about Me; and yet you are unwilling to come to Me so that you may have life." (John 5:39-40, NASB)

So, if you truly want a transformed life, here are three daily practices we encourage you to commit to:

1 Commit to daily worship and prayer

Set aside a regular time each day to focus on God. Some people call this a 'quiet time'. Whether it's first thing in the morning, last thing at night or anytime in between, find a time that works best for you and commit to it.

In your quiet time, before you jump into a list of prayer requests, start your time with praise, worship and thanksgiving (see Philippians 4:4-7).

Remember prayer is not just a one-way communication, it's a dialogue with God (See: John 10:27 and John 16:13). He wants to speak to you. So, it is important to give time to simply be quiet before Him, to listen, to wait in His presence (see Psalm 46:10).

2 Commit to daily Bible reading

"… man does not live on bread alone but on every word that comes from the mouth of the Lord." (Deuteronomy 8:3, NIV)

Just as our body everyday needs food to keep going, so our inner person – our soul and spirit – needs spiritual food to grow, get stronger and keep going. The Bible is spiritual food.

Tips for reading the Bible:

- Have a reading plan. The You Version Bible App has a number of plans you can choose from.
- Start with the basics. If you are new to reading the Bible, we would recommend starting with one of the Gospels, such as Luke or John, and then read Acts. The Psalms and Proverbs are also excellent to dip in and out of.
- Quality is more important than quantity. It is better to read less and for it to have an impact than feeling the pressure to read lots of chapters and not take it in.
- Ask God to speak to you every time you read.

3 Commit to do what His word says

"… whoever looks intently into the perfect law that gives freedom and continues in it - not forgetting what they have heard, but doing it - they will be blessed in what they do." (James 1:25, NIV)

The key to being "blessed" in every area of life is to do what the Bible says in every area of your life. Let God's word direct your relationships, your finances, your decisions, your private life and your public life. This is what it means to be a follower of Jesus.

The good news is, the more you spend time in the Bible the more you become like its author.

FREQUENTLY ASKED QUESTIONS

HOW DO WE KNOW THAT THE BIBLE HAS NOT BEEN WATERED DOWN THROUGH CENTURIES OF TRANSLATION?

This is a question that many sceptics, atheists and even Muslims commonly raise to challenge the credibility of the modern Bible. Indeed Dan Brown, the author of the 'Da Vinci Code' says: "The Bible ... has evolved through countless translations, additions, and revisions. History has never had a definitive version of the book."

There are three reasons you can trust our modern Bible translations:

1 The quality and quantity of available ancient manuscripts

Here are what some of the experts have said about the New Testament:

Amy Orr-Ewing, in her book, 'Why trust the Bible', writes:

"There are more than 5300 known Greek manuscripts of the New Testament. Add 10,000 Latin manuscripts and 9,300 early portions of the New Testament, and we have around 24,000 existent manuscript copies of portions of the New Testament. No other document from antiquity approaches this."

"There is no body of ancient literature in the world which enjoys such a wealth of good textual attestation as the New Testament." (F. F. Bruce)

"To be sceptical ... of the New Testament books is to allow all of classical antiquity to slip into obscurity, for no documents of the ancient period are as well attested bibliographically as the New Testament." (John Warwick Montgomery)

2 External references

Many 1st Century non-biblical writings directly quote excerpts from the New Testament. These writings give us an ancient means of corroborating the accuracy of our modern New Testament translations. Again, Amy Orr-Ewing says:

"... a further witness to the New Testament is found in the thousands of quotations which are dispersed throughout the writings of the church Fathers. In fact, there are 86,000 quotations - this means that if all the ancient New Testament manuscripts were somehow to disappear overnight, it would still be possible to reconstruct the entire New Testament with quotations from the church Fathers, with the exception of about twenty verses!"

Many non-Christian writers from early centuries also attest to the people, places, and events recorded in the New Testament.

3 The Dead Sea Scrolls

In 1947 a shepherd boy in the wilderness near the Dead Sea discovered large pottery jars with rolls of scrolls in the inner recesses of a cave. The scrolls were 1900-year-old copies of the Old Testament, minus the book of Esther. Scholars compared these ancient copies of the scripture to modern translations to see if any changes had occurred through generations of translation. They found that there were virtually no variations other than some changes to grammar and punctuation, which did not change the meaning or impact of scripture.

IS THE BIBLE HISTORICALLY ACCURATE?

The Bible is true history: real people, real places, real times. How do we know this? The same way you know that any other history is accurate. A historian would ask if the text has been written by somebody who saw the event in question or is it second-hand or third-hand testimony, or is it a legend written down hundreds of years later?

Take the Gospels for example. Luke – whose Gospel dates from 58-60AD, making it the last one written – starts his account with an air of historical credibility:

> "Many have undertaken to draw up an account of the things that have been fulfilled among us, just as they were handed down to us by those who from the first were eyewitnesses and servants of the word. With this in mind, since I myself have carefully investigated everything from the beginning, I too decided to write an orderly account for you, most excellent Theophilus, so that you may know the certainty of the things you have been taught." (Luke 1:1-4, NIV)

Matthew and Mark wrote their Gospels within a decade of the crucifixion when the events were still fresh in their minds. Matthew was a tax collector, a profession that demanded the knowledge of three languages and their own form of shorthand, which made it possible to keep notes on the events as they unfolded.

Also, Jesus spoke in memorable ways using parables and often provocative statements. Jesus' life was so dramatic that its events would be emblazoned on the minds of the early apostles - the blind seeing, lame walking, storms stopping and even the dead rising.

The Gospel accounts of the resurrection are recorded in a matter-of-fact, brief, non-dramatic, and factual historical way. The Gospel writers recount that the first witnesses of the resurrection were women, which at that time would have discredited the miracle as a women's testimony in 1st Century Palestine counted for little. That most of the apostles would die as martyrs for the truths they were writing about adds an immense weight to their testimony - who would live and die for a lie?

Outside of the Christian community there were many other 1st Century historians and writers who chronicled events from the New Testament such as Tacitus, Josephus, Suetonius, and the Roman governor Pliny the Younger. While these writers did not necessarily agree with the message of Jesus and the Christians, they did not disagree with the historicity of the accounts. There are at least 45 historical references by Roman, Jewish and pagan writers who confirmed that:

- Jesus was a wonder worker
- He gathered a group of disciples
- He was executed under Pontius Pilate
- There was an eclipse of the sun at the crucifixion
- His disciples preached that He had risen
- Christianity spread rapidly

"I am a Jew, but I am enthralled by the luminous figure of the Nazarene … No one can read the Gospels without feeling the actual presence of Jesus. His personality pulsates in every word. No myth is filled with such life." (Albert Einstein)

The Bible's accuracy is confirmed by archeology. Here are two examples:

For centuries historians questioned the existence of Solomon. Many were certain he did not have horses, as the biblical accounts say, as kings at that time and location only had camels. And then, at Megiddo in northern Israel, archaeologists discovered one of Solomon's chariot cities with thousands of stables for horses.

In John's Gospel we read "Now there is in Jerusalem near the Sheep Gate a pool, which in Aramaic is called Bethesda and which is surrounded by five covered colonnades." (John 5:2, NIV). Bible sceptics argued that there was never any record of such a pool existing in that part of Jerusalem. However, in the late 19th Century archaeologists discovered the remains of the pool and sure enough it had "five covered colonnades."

The Bible is scientifically accurate. In fact, the Bible put into writing many things that only were scientifically understood relatively recently. As Johannes Kepler, the famous mathematician and astronomer, best known for his laws of planetary motion, said: "Science is simply thinking God's thoughts after him."

The ancient world did not believe the Earth was suspended in space but rather on pillars or people, such as the depiction of Atlas in Greek mythology or animals in Hinduism. Job, the oldest book in the Bible and possibly the oldest book in existence, says: "... he suspends the earth over nothing." (Job 26:7, NIV)

The water cycle was not fully understood until about 30BC by a Roman engineer, Marcus Vitruvius. Yet for thousands of years before the Bible had described this process (Ecclesiastes 1:6-7; 11:3; Job 26:8; Amos 9:6).

For centuries the prevailing scientific thought was that there were about a thousand stars in the universe and that they could be counted. In 150BC a man named Hipparchus did just that and wrote a famous dissertation saying that there were 1022 stars in the universe. 300 years later, Ptolemy repeated the exercise and counted 1026. He found four more stars! However, it is widely accepted today that there are more stars in the universe than there are grains of sand on the planet earth. Some 2600 years ago in the Bible God said this: "... as the stars of the sky cannot be counted and the sand on the seashore cannot be measured ..." (Jeremiah 33:22, NLT)

For thousands of years, people erroneously believed the earth was flat, until Copernicus, Galileo and Columbus challenged this belief. If the Bible was of human origin, you would expect it to repeat this received wisdom of the time. Yet 2600 years ago Isaiah said: "He sits enthroned above the circle of the earth ..." (Isaiah 40:22, NIV)

The Bible is prophetically accurate. When considering the life of Jesus, Dr. Charles Ryrie says that according to the laws of chance, it would require 200 billion earths, populated with four billion people each, to come up with one person whose life could fulfil 100 accurate prophecies without any errors in sequence. Yet the Scriptures record not 100, but more than 300 prophecies that were fulfilled in Christ's first coming alone.

Take the Old Testament book of Daniel, for example. He accurately predicted many world events, which are now recorded in our history books. Here are some examples:

- The fall of Babylon
- The rise and fall of the Media-Persian Empire
- The emergence and rapid advance of the Greek Empire
- The prominent leader of the Greek Empire, Alexander the Great, his premature death, and the fact that he was replaced by his four generals
- The emergence of the Roman Empire
- The virgin birth of Jesus at the time of the Roman Empire
- The time of Jesus' arrival in Jerusalem prior to His crucifixion (see Daniel 9:25)
- The rise of the church and its global impact (see Daniel 2)

Many critics argue that Daniel must have been written in retrospect and not by Daniel himself. However, we know that the Septuagint – the Greek version of the Hebrew Old Testament – was published around 250BC, which was prior to and in the midst of many of above prophecies being fulfilled, and it contained the book of Daniel. Indeed, Josephus records that the book of Daniel was shown to Alexander the Great when he approached the city of Jerusalem around 331 BC. Also, Ezekiel 14:14, 20, which was written between 586 and 538 BC, refers to Daniel.

IS THE APOCRYPHA SCRIPTURE?

Catholicism includes seven additional books between the Old and New Testaments. These books relate to the so-called '400 years of silence' between the end of the Old Testament and the coming of Jesus as recorded in the New Testament. While the Apocrypha is an interesting historical read, it was neither considered as scripture by the Jews of Jesus' day, nor by the early church. Likewise, we do not consider the Apocrypha as God-inspired scripture today. Here are some reasons why:

- According to the Talmud, the Jewish view of the Apocrypha is that: "After the latter prophets Haggai, Zechariah and Malachi the Holy Spirit departed from Israel."
- The Jewish 1st Century historian Josephus says that a copy of the Hebrew scriptures was preserved in the temple in Jerusalem. He lists the 39 books in the scriptures, the same as our Old Testament and not including the books of the Apocrypha.
- Jesus said: "... this generation will be held responsible for the blood of all the prophets that has been shed since the beginning of the world, from the blood of Abel to the blood of Zechariah, who was killed between the altar and the sanctuary. Yes, I tell you, this generation will be held responsible for it all." (Luke 11:50-51, NIV). In saying this, Jesus was referring to the entire Old Testament. Zechariah was the last martyr listed in the Jewish Old Testament, which appeared in a different book order from the Christian Old Testament. Jesus clearly understood that the Apocrypha wasn't considered part of the canon of scripture.
- The early Christian church did not include the Apocrypha in the Bible. It was only in 1546 in reaction to the Reformation that the Roman Catholic Church at the Council of Trent decided to give canonical – or biblical – status to the Apocrypha.

HOW CAN YOU SAY THAT YOU HAVE THE RIGHT INTERPRETATION OF SCRIPTURE? ARE ALL INTERPRETATIONS NOT EQUALLY VALID?

The church father, Augustine, once said:

> "If you believe what you like in the Bible, and reject what you like, it's not the Bible you believe but yourself."

As humans, we tend to see everything through the lens of our options and preferences. But when it comes to the Bible as God's word, it is important we approach the text with a humble and teachable attitude, not imposing our views but instead seeking to know God's.

Hermeneutics, the science of interpreting scripture, gives us several key principles which, when applied, help us come to an accurate understanding of what the Bible is teaching:

1 Read the text in its context

When seeking to understand a statement in the Bible ask yourself what role this sentence plays in this paragraph, chapter or the broader argument of the book?

For example, in Psalm 51 David says: "Behold, I was brought forth in iniquity, and in sin my mother conceived me." (Psalm 51:5, NASB). Is David talking about his sin or is he referring to a sin his mother committed? Maybe she had an affair? When you look at the context of the entire Psalm, you discover it is all about David's sin, so we can safely conclude that in this verse David referring to himself – like all of us - being born with a sinful nature.

2 Understand the historical and geographical context

There is a wealth of information from the ancient world, including archaeological finds and historic writings from both secular and religious authors.

For example, in the book of Revelation Jesus addresses the church at Laodicea:

> "To the angel of the church in Laodicea write … I know your deeds, that you are neither cold nor hot. I wish you were either one or the other! So, because you are lukewarm—neither hot nor cold—I am about to spit you out of my mouth." (Revelation 3:14-16, NIV)

Archaeologists have discovered that Laodicea's water supply was channeled from hot springs some distance away and by the time the water reached the town the hot water had become tepid. This bit of context helps us understand more deeply the challenge that Jesus was bringing to the church.

3 Look at the original language

The New Testament was written in Greek and the Old Testament was written mainly in Hebrew. Looking at the original languages can help you deepen your understanding of a passage. There are many resources in print and online to help you discover the meaning of the original Greek or Hebrew words.

Here is an example of how a study of the original language helps you understand the meaning of a verse. In Exodus 20:13 we read the commandment, "you shall not kill". What does this mean? Some people take this to mean that we are forbidden to swat flies, step on an ant or eat meat. Others have used this verse to argue you should not fight in war. The Hebrew word for 'kill' used in this verse is 'ratsach'. This word occurs between 30 and 40 times in the Old Testament. On no occasion, is it used in reference to killing an insect or killing a person in battle. The word is always used in reference to premeditated murder or taking a life through carelessness. So, the commandment specifically means 'you shall not murder', i.e., manslaughter.

4 Understand the unclear in the light of the clear

We believe that "The sum of Your word is truth ..." (Psalm 119:160, NASB). In other words, when the Bible is put all together it is consistent and does not contradict itself. Because God is author of it all, each individual verse will be consistent with the meaning of the whole book. With this in mind, always interpret the unclear statements of the Bible in the light of the clear.

A classic example of when this principle is important is when considering if infant baptism is appropriate based on the verse "he [the jailer] and all his household were baptised." (Acts 16:33). Some people might argue that there might have been very young children in this family who were being baptised. But when you look elsewhere at clearer verses in scripture you discover, without exception, that baptism always comes in response to a person consciously repenting and believing - something a baby can't do (see: Mark 16:16, Matthew 28:19, Acts 2:38). If you apply the principle reading the text in its context, a few verses earlier, in Acts 16:31, show that before being baptised the instruction from the apostles was "Believe in the Lord Jesus, and you will be saved -

you and your household". In other words, the whole family being baptised came after the whole family believing in Jesus.

5 Consider continuity or discontinuity

There are certain practices and commands in the Old Testament that no longer apply to us as we move into the New Testament era because they have been fulfilled in Christ. At the same time, other principles continue through both the Old and New Testaments.

Here are two examples of practices which have been discontinued:

- There is no longer a requirement to present sacrifices for our sins, because Jesus once and for all time was sacrificed for our sin (see Hebrews 10)
- We no longer need to circumcise our male children, because baptism is now the initiation into the family of God (see Colossians 2:11-12)

Here are two examples of continuity:

- The principle of bringing the tithe to God continues as a principle to follow – but not a legalistic requirement – as Abraham, operating in faith, tithed before the law came into being
- Similarly, the practice of observing a weekly Sabbath pre-dates the law. So while we no longer are required to legalistically obey the Sabbath laws, it remains a wise principle to follow. Both put God first in the earthly resources of time (the Sabbath) and money (tithing).

6 Interpret scripture bearing in mind that the central figure of the entire Bible is Jesus

Both the Old and the New Testaments are about Jesus! Jesus is in the Old Testament concealed but in the New Testament He is revealed.

Jesus said to the Old Testament scholars of His time: "You search the Scriptures because you think that in them you have eternal life; it is these that testify about Me; and you are unwilling to come to Me so that you may have life." (John 5:39-40, NASB)

After the resurrection Jesus took two of His disciples on a tour of the Old Testament scriptures: "beginning with Moses and all the Prophets, he explained to them what was said in all the Scriptures concerning himself." (Luke 24:27, NIV)

It is as if there is a large cross placed between the Old and New Testaments. In the light of the New Testament, we see the shadow of the cross being cast throughout the pages of the Old.

THE GOSPEL AND OUR RESPONSE

"I am not ashamed of the gospel, for it is the power of God for salvation to everyone who believes ..." (Romans 1:16, NASB)

The word "gospel" means good news and indeed the message of Jesus is very good news. To fully appreciate the good news, we first need to understand the bad news, and to understand the bad news we need to go right back to the beginning when things went wrong.

In the beginning, God created a perfect world and into this perfect world, He placed mankind, created in the very image of God. We were created to know and glorify God. Tragically in Genesis 3, we read that Satan, a rebellious fallen angel, successfully tempted our first parents to sin. This is called the fall of man and it changed everything. We became sinners, the world became corrupted, and suffering and death became normal. Worst of all, we became separated from God, the very source of life.

THE ROMANS ROAD

The following verses from the book of Romans clearly describe the journey of our fall and what God did to save us. Some people call this progression of verses "The Romans Road."

"... all have sinned and fall short of the glory of God ..." (Romans 3:23, NASB)

We all have something in common, we're all sinners. This is the bad news. Whether you are rich or poor, educated or uneducated, religious or atheist - "all have sinned."

Even though it was Adam and Eve that sinned in the beginning, every human since has inherited the same fallen and sinful nature. This means that we are sinners by nature as well as by choice. No one is innocent.

Imagine you conducted a survey asking, "Are people fundamentally good or evil?" Most responses would be something like: "I know we're not perfect, but I believe people are fundamentally good." While we would all like to believe this, the truth of the Bible is that we are fundamentally evil and sinful (see Romans 3:10-18).

About a century ago The Times newspaper in London ran a series of articles asking big questions. One was, "What's wrong with the world?". The Catholic writer G. K. Chesterton, known for his directness and sharp answers, replied to the editors:

"Dear Sirs: I am. Sincerely Yours, G. K. Chesterton."

He was absolutely right. The problem in the world is not political, social or economic. We all want to point at a circumstance or an individual out there. But the Bible teaches us that our problem is on the inside. Sin is the root behind all the bad fruit on earth, all the suffering, the injustice, the disease and the grief. The heart of the human problem is the problem of the human heart.

The Romans Road goes on to tell us the consequence of our sin.

"... the wages of sin is death ..." (Romans 6:23, NIV)

In Genesis God warned Adam and Eve "... from the tree of the knowledge of good and evil you shall not eat, for on the day that you eat from it you will certainly die." (Genesis 2:17, NASB). However, Adam and Eve, having eaten the forbidden fruit, did not drop dead. In fact, they continued living for an extremely long time. What then did God mean by "you will certainly die"?

The New Testament explains: "... in Adam all die, so in Christ all will be made alive." (1 Corinthians 15:22, NIV). There are only two types of people on earth. You are either 'in Adam' by just being born, or you are 'in Christ' by having been born-again.

The gospel message of Jesus does not take bad people and make them into good people - it is far worse than that and far better than that. It takes dead people and makes them into people who are alive!

Sin brought spiritual death, which by necessity leads to physical death.

Being spiritually dead means we are disconnected from God (see Isaiah 59:2, Ephesians 2:12). This disconnection from God causes people to seek spiritual answers, sometimes in the wrong places. We know we were created for something more.

The French philosopher and mathematician, Blaise Pascal described our condition very well when he wrote: "There is a God-shaped vacuum inside every human heart."

Augustine echoed this same idea, declaring: "We are made for You, O God, and our hearts are restless until they have found their rest in You."

The bad news just gets worse. Our spiritual deadness not only causes our inevitable physical death; it also leads to eternal death and separation from God. The Bible calls this hell.

> "When all is done, the hell of hells, the torment of torments, is the everlasting absence of God, and the everlasting impossibility of returning to his presence... to fall out of the hands of the living God, is a horror beyond our expression, beyond our imagination." (John Donne, a poet and lawyer, in 1622)

But now here comes the good news ...

"... the wages of sin is death, but the gift of God is eternal life in Christ Jesus our Lord." (Romans 6:23, NIV)

Sin has a wage that needs to be paid, and that wage is death. But the good news is that Jesus paid our wages for us, He died the death we should have died.

You may have heard of identity theft. Identity theft happens when someone assumes your identity and amasses debt against you. What Jesus did on the cross was similar, but it accomplished a hugely positive result. On the cross, Jesus assumed our identity, but instead of amassing debt against us, He cleared our moral debt and died our death. Jesus literally died in our place!

> "... we do see Jesus, who was made lower than the angels for a little while, now crowned with glory and honour because he suffered death, so that by the grace of God he might taste death for everyone." (Hebrews 2:9, NIV)

> "... Christ also died for sins once for all, the just for the unjust, so that He might bring us to God..." (1 Peter 3:18, NASB)

In Hinduism karma demands: "If you sin, you pay." But in the gospel God says: "You sin, I pay!"

The essence of sin is us substituting ourselves for God - we try to be our own god - but the essence of salvation is God substituting Himself for us.

He was punished, so we will not be punished (see John 5:24).

He was condemned, so we will never be condemned (see Romans 8:1).

He became sin, so we can become the righteousness of God (see: 2 Corinthians 5:21).

He was willing to go through hell for us, because He was unwilling to go to heaven without us (see John 3:16).

Someone accurately summed up God's grace in this way: G.R.A.C.E. stands for: God's Riches At Christ's Expense.

So how do we receive this gift of eternal life?

"... if you confess with your mouth Jesus as Lord, and believe in your heart that God raised Him from the dead, you will be saved ..." (Romans 10:9, NASB)

The human race was lost when we, through Adam and Eve in the beginning, rejected His rule over our lives. It is no surprise then that our salvation comes when we at last surrender to God and confess "Jesus as our Lord."

In that verse from Romans 10, the Greek word used for "believe" is "pistis" which means a firm persuasion. To believe in the resurrection is to believe in what Christ achieved and completed on the cross. It is having a firm persuasion that what Jesus did in dying and rising is sufficient to save your soul. Someone once described faith as our responsibility - it's our response to His ability to save us.

"Upon a life I did not live,

Upon a death I did not die;

Another's life, another's death,

I stake my whole eternity."

("Upon a life I did not live," hymn by Horatius Bonar)

"Therefore, having been justified by faith, we have peace with God through our Lord Jesus Christ ..." (Romans 5:1, NASB)

As we trust in Jesus' saving work on the cross and in His resurrection, the Bible describes us as being "justified." This is a legal word used in a courtroom. Being justified is when a judge declares the person on trial "not guilty," and they walk free.

"... to the one who does not work but trusts God who justifies the ungodly, their faith is credited as righteousness." (Romans 4:5, NIV)

A human judge who ignored the evidence and acquitted the guilty would be no longer fit to serve as a judge. So how can God, who is perfectly just, ignore our sin and declare us not guilty, when clearly, we are sinners? The answer is, that God didn't ignore our sin. On the contrary, He personally paid the penalty for our sins and died on our behalf. In this act both His justice and His love were satisfied.

"Ponder the achievement of God. He doesn't condone our sin; nor does he compromise his standard. He doesn't ignore our rebellion; nor does he relax his demands. Rather than dismiss our sin he assumes our sin and, incredibly, sentences himself. God's holiness is honoured. Our sin is punished. And we are redeemed. God is still God. The wages of sin is still death. And we are made perfect." (Max Lucado)

He didn't just clear our moral debt, He credited to our account His own righteousness.

"He made Him who knew no sin to be sin on our behalf, so that we might become the righteousness of God in Him." (2 Corinthians 5:21, NASB)

For Christians, righteousness is not a quality that is in our lives. Our behaviour is often unrighteous. Our righteousness is a resurrected Saviour in heaven today. He is in us, and we are in Him. He is our righteousness. Through Jesus we are loved, righteous, holy, eternally accepted and pleasing to God. Just as Jesus is loved and welcomed by the Father, so now we, who are "in Him," are accepted before the Father. Truly "… he has blessed us in the Beloved." (Ephesians 1:6, ESV)

"So near, so very near to God,

I cannot nearer be;

For in the person of His Son

I am as near as He.

So dear, so very dear to God,

More dear I cannot be;

The love wherewith He loves the Son;

Such is His love to me!"

"Peace with God" is not just a new relationship with God we enjoy in this life, it is an eternal reality. Most people think of heaven simply as a place that you go to when you die, but at a deeper level in essence heaven is the eternal state of being in relationship with God (see John 17:3). When someone is saved, they are from that point forward they are eternally connected with God. When a saved person dies, they simply entered into the full experience of this relationship. As Paul said: "For now we see only a reflection as in a mirror; then we shall see face to face. Now I know in part; then I shall know fully, even as I am fully known." (1 Corinthians 13:12, NIV).

"The gospel is not a way to get people to heaven; it is a way to get people to God. It's a way of overcoming every obstacle to everlasting joy in God. If we don't want God above all things, we have not been converted by the gospel." (John Piper)

In summary, the good news (the gospel) is:

We are all sinful and therefore separated from God. We can do nothing to save ourselves from this predicament. God in His love for us did what we could not do. He paid the price for our sins and made it possible for us to again be in relationship with God. By trusting in Jesus and His death in our place and resurrection, we receive forgiveness for our sins and enter into this new and eternal relationship with God.

OUR RESPONSE TO THE GOOD NEWS

It is our faith in Jesus that saves us. But genuine saving faith is not passive and inactive. Many people claim to have faith, but their lives remain unchanged. This is not saving faith.

> "What good is it, dear brothers and sisters, if you say you have faith but don't show it by your actions? Can that kind of faith save anyone?" (James 2:14, NLT)

"As the body without the spirit is dead, so faith without deeds is dead."
(James 2:26, NIV)

To be very clear, it is not faith plus works that saves us. That is called legalism. Rather it is faith that works which saves us.

Our desire is to build our lives and churches on biblical foundations. With this in mind, let us look at the record in Acts to see how people coming to Christ expressed their genuine saving faith.

Acts chapter 2 records a pivotal moment in world history - the birth of the church. It was the Jewish festival of Pentecost, seven weeks had passed since the resurrection of Jesus, and God had just dramatically poured out His Spirit on the disciples gathered in Jerusalem. A huge crowd gathered to witness the phenomena, so the apostle Peter stood up to address the multitudes. The Bible records their response as he explained the gospel:

> "When the people heard this, they were cut to the heart and said to Peter and the other apostles, "Brothers, what shall we do?" Peter replied, **"Repent and be baptised,** every one of you, in the name of Jesus Christ for the forgiveness of your sins. And **you will receive the gift of the Holy Spirit.** The promise is for you and your children and for all who are far off - for all whom the Lord our God will call." With many other words he warned them; and he pleaded with them, "Save yourselves from this corrupt generation." Those who accepted his message were baptised, and about three thousand were added to their number that day." (Acts 2:37-41, NIV)

The apostle Peter is clear - if you want to follow Jesus you have to:

- **Repent**
- **Be baptised**
- **And receive the gift of the Holy Spirit**

We see the same faith steps being followed time after time in the book of Acts (see: Acts 8:4-17, 9:17-18, 10:44-48, 19:1-6)

The writer of Hebrews refers to repentance, baptism and receiving the Holy Spirit - what they call the "laying on of hands" - as a "foundation" in a believer's life.

"Therefore, leaving the discussion of the elementary principles of Christ, let us go on to perfection, not laying again the foundation of repentance from dead works and of faith toward God, of the doctrine of baptisms, of laying on of hands…" (Hebrews 6:1-2, NKJV)

In a construction project, the foundation is the first thing to be put in place. It determines the strength and the stability of the building. These three steps of faith and obedience are the foundations for every believer, providing a strong start for the journey that lies ahead.

Today many believers have believed but haven't properly repented and are still tolerating sin in their lives. Others have repented but have yet to be baptised. And there are still others who have not experienced being filled with the Holy Spirit.

So, with authentic faith in Jesus let's commit to putting these foundations in place in our lives.

1 BELIEVE IN JESUS AND REPENT OF YOUR SIN

Faith and repentance go hand-in-hand. It would be strange for someone who truly believes that Jesus had to die to take away their sins to then continue to embrace and justify the very sin that nailed Him to the cross. The famous 19th Century London preacher Charles Spurgeon vividly makes this point:

"If I had a brother who had been murdered, what would you think of me if I … daily consorted with the assassin who drove the dagger into my brother's heart; surely, I too must be an accomplice in the crime. Sin murdered Christ; will you be a friend to it? Sin pierced the heart of the Incarnate God; can you love it?"

Many people think that to repent primarily means to change your behaviour. But actually, the Greek word for repentance - "metanoeó" - means to change your mind. Repentance is a change of mind that leads to a change of behaviour.

Are you willing to change your mind about sin?

Are you willing to reject the sins that you like and enjoy?

Are you willing to change your mind and reject lifestyles that the Bible calls sinful and embrace God's ways?

Here are some sins the Bible calls us to repent from:

- Occult or New Age involvement (see: Acts 19:18-20)
- Pride, self-sufficiency and lust (see: 1 John 2:16)
- Greed, sexual sins, theft and idolatry (see: 1 Corinthians 6:9-11)

Repentance is not just concerned with stopping bad behaviour; it is equally passionate about pursuing right living.

Remember, good behaviour is not what saves you. Your good works are not the root of your salvation, they are the fruit of your salvation. We have not been saved by good works, but for good works, as Paul writes in Ephesians:

> "For by grace you have been saved through faith; and this is not of yourselves, it is the gift of God; not a result of works, so that no one may boast. For we are His workmanship, created in Christ Jesus for good works, which God prepared beforehand so that we would walk in them." (Ephesians 2:8-10, NASB)

Like any foundation, repentance is there at the beginning of your journey with God but is just as essential in the years that follow. Repentance is to be an ongoing attitude throughout our lives, an attitude of submitting to God and choosing to live in His will. It is an attitude that remains even when we fail - as we will many times (see Proverbs 24:16). When you fail remember you cannot lose through bad works that which you did not gain through good works. Pick yourself up, turn back to God, receive

His forgiveness and start walking again. The failure is not the person who falls down; it is the person who stays down.

2 BE BAPTISED

Baptism in scripture was the next expression of a believers' newfound faith. It is a powerful act by which a person buries their old self.

In the Old Testament we find a foreshadowing of Christian baptism in the account of Israel's exodus from Egypt:

> "All of them were guided by a cloud that moved ahead of them, and all of them walked through the sea on dry ground. In the cloud and in the sea, all of them were baptised as followers of Moses." (1 Corinthians 10:1-2, NLT)

- Just as Moses was used to set the Israelites free from their slavery in Egypt, so too Jesus has set us free from our spiritual slavery to sin.
- Straight after gaining their freedom the Israelites had to pass through the Red Sea to cut off the past and bury the Egyptian army. So too, as believers we bury and break the hold of our past by being baptised.
- As the Israelites were guided through their journey by following God's presence in the cloud, so too believers have been given the gift of the Holy Spirit to fill us and guide us into our purpose.

Before the word was used in a Christian context, baptism was used to describe the process by which a cloth was immersed in a vat of dye and would come out a new colour. So, it is clear that baptism is not merely a symbolic act. It is a moment when our past is dealt with, and we are changed.

In various Christian traditions, the word baptism has come to mean many things. For some baptism is a sprinkling with water. For others, it is a decision parents make on behalf of their children when they are infants. In this study, we are interested primarily in what God's word says. Above any particular tradition, our allegiance is to God and His revealed pattern as found in scripture. With this approach in mind let's look at what the Bible teaches.

The word baptise ("baptizō" in Greek) means to immerse or submerge. So when Peter said: "Repent and be baptised ..." he was instructing new believers to repent and be submerged in water.

There are 31 references in the New Testament to baptism and all of them without exception refer to people getting baptised who have first repented and believed (as opposed to infants who have yet to make a personal response to the gospel).

In conclusion, God's pattern in scripture is that new believers (of any age) should get baptised by full immersion.

To be very clear, baptism is not what saves you - it is your faith in Jesus that saves you. For example, in response to the faith of the thief on the cross beside Him, Jesus turned to him and said, "today you shall be with Me in paradise" (Luke 23:43). The thief was not saved by any good work or by being baptised, he was saved purely on trusting the man on the cross next to him! Baptism is not essential for getting you to heaven, but it is essential for living free on earth. The Bible teacher Ern Baxter nails it when he said: "You don't need to be baptised to be saved, but you do need to be baptised to be obedient."

> "Those who accepted his message were baptised, and about three thousand were added to their number that day." (Acts 2:41, NIV)

We read here and elsewhere in Acts that the new believers were baptised immediately. The apostles did not wait a few weeks to see if the new believers' conversions were genuine. They did not make them attend a baptism class. They simply baptised them. So don't delay any longer - if you are a believer, be baptised.

3 RECEIVE THE GIFT OF THE HOLY SPIRIT

"Repent and be baptised, every one of you, in the name of Jesus Christ for the forgiveness of your sins. And you will receive the gift of the Holy Spirit." (Acts 2:38)

Repentance and baptisms are steps that we take but receiving "the gift of the Holy Spirit" is a generous act of God. Notice the Holy Spirit is referred to as a "gift." The Holy Spirit is not earned by our good behaviour or maturity. He comes as a gift of God in response to our faith in Jesus (see Galatians 3:5).

The Bible is clear that every believer receives the gift of the Holy Spirit at the point of conversion. Indeed, the work of conversion itself is a work of the Spirit (see Romans 8:15). But the Bible is also clear that every believer can have an experience called baptism with the Holy Spirit, and this experience is typically separate from conversion (see Acts 8:14-16). We will look at the baptism with the Holy Spirit in the next study.

The Holy Spirit comes to guide and help us in life.

Jesus said: "I will ask the Father, and He will give you another Helper, so that He may be with you forever ..." (John 14:16, NASB)

The original Greek word for "Helper" is the word "Parakletos," which is made up of two words "kletos" (to call) and "para" (alongside). Jesus is telling us that the Holy Spirit is called to walk alongside us to help us through life's journey - you are no longer alone.

The Holy Spirit comes to empower us to tell others the good news.

Jesus said: "... you will receive power when the Holy Spirit has come upon you; and you shall be My witnesses both in Jerusalem, and in all Judea and Samaria, and even to the remotest part of the earth." (Acts 1:8, NASB)

How effective we are at telling others about Jesus doesn't come from our communication skills, our clever arguments, or our dramatic stories. The Holy Spirit works through us to convince and convert others, all He needs is our willingness to speak and He will do the rest.

Like the crowd in Jerusalem who heard the gospel 2000 years ago on Pentecost, we have also heard the good news of salvation available in Jesus. In the same way they wholeheartedly responded, we are also called to respond with faith, repentance, a decision to get baptised and a receptivity to the Holy Spirit. These are the foundations we build our lives upon.

FREQUENTLY ASKED QUESTIONS

WILL PEOPLE WHO NEVER HEAR THE GOSPEL GO TO HEAVEN?

There are some questions that only God can answer. Only God can decide the eternal destiny of a human being. However, God has made some things clear to us in the Bible:

- There are not many ways to God - Jesus is the only Saviour. (see John 14:6, Acts 4:12)
- While the Bible acknowledges that not everyone will be saved (see Matthew 7:13), it is also clear that God "desires all people to be saved and to come to the knowledge of the truth." (1 Timothy 2:4, ESV) And again: "he is patient with you, not wanting anyone to perish, but everyone to come to repentance." (2 Peter 3:9, NIV)
- The Bible is clear that people who know the truth and reject will be judged more severely than those who did not know. (see Luke 12:47-48)
- We can be sure that God is good and just in all His dealings. (see Psalm 89:14)
- The Bible is full of examples of God reaching people who were far from Him: He sends Philip to an Ethiopian eunuch (see Acts

8), He appears to Saul in a vision (see Acts 9), He sends an angel and then the apostle Peter to the Roman centurion Cornelius (see Acts 10)

Today there is testimony from many Muslims who have converted to Christianity after having a vision of Jesus.

We know many stories of people who, like the thief on the Cross, turn to Jesus in the last moments of their lives.

Here are two more helpful and motivating questions for us to consider:

- Now that you know the gospel, have you responded in faith and repentance?
- If you have accepted Jesus, are you telling others the good news?

WHAT IS HEAVEN REALLY LIKE?

There is so much emphasis today in Christian circles on people going to heaven when they die. It is not uncommon to hear preachers exhorting people to believe in Jesus to be guaranteed heaven in the afterlife. The typical Christian would think of heaven as a mysterious unphysical place in another realm where they will spend eternity with God. It might surprise you to discover that this concept of heaven is not what the New Testament portrays as the ultimate destination of God's people.

It is true that believers will go immediately to heaven when they die. When their body dies their spirit is very much alive and in the presence of God. Paul describes looking forward to this reality: "I desire to depart and be with Christ…" (Philippians 1:23, NIV). Elsewhere he says he desires "…to be away from the body and at home with the Lord." (2 Corinthians 5:8, NIV). However, God's design and intention for us was never to exist as disembodied spirits in heaven. Instead, He designed us as beings who have a spirit, soul and body (see 1 Thessalonians 5:23) and who live on earth as our domain (see Psalm 115:16 and Matthew 5:5).

In Genesis chapter 3 we discover that when man sinned in the fall, death came into the world. Sin not only brought spiritual death but also eventual physical death. As we have learned, the good news is that Jesus came to bring the great reversal and ultimately to conquer death itself.

> "For since death came through a man, the resurrection of the dead comes also through a man. For as in Adam all die, so in Christ all will be made alive." (1 Corinthians 15:21-22, NIV)

In salvation, God's plan isn't just to make us alive spiritually. God's plan is a full reversal of the consequences of the fall. God plans to resurrect us in spirit, soul and body. Coming alive on the inside and going to heaven when we die is just the beginning.

From the New Testament, we understand that there is a present heaven, where believers who have passed away currently reside. This is an intermediary heaven, which exists until the great final resurrection takes place.

The Bible is clear that ultimately God will raise His people physically from the dead just as Jesus Himself rose (see Job 19:25-27, Daniel 12:2-3, 1 Corinthians 15:42-52, 1 Thessalonians 4:14-16). Then death will truly be defeated. Death is not defeated just because we go to heaven when we die. Death is defeated because we will rise again with immortal bodies never to die again.

After Jesus returns, not only will believers have resurrected bodies, but the whole earth will be in effect resurrected. At last, we will see the final part of the great reversal. As the curse is removed from earth and death, sin and Satan himself are done away with.

> "Then I saw "a new heaven and a new earth," for the first heaven and the first earth had passed away, and there was no longer any sea. I saw the Holy City, the new Jerusalem, coming down out of heaven from God, prepared as a bride beautifully dressed for her husband. And I heard a loud voice from the throne saying, "Look! God's dwelling place is now among the people, and he will dwell with them. They will be his people, and God himself will be with them and be their God. 'He will wipe every tear from their eyes. There will be no more death' or mourning or crying or pain, for the old order of things has passed away." He who was seated

on the throne said, "I am making everything new!"" (Revelation 21:1-5, NIV)

The ultimate heaven will not be in another non-physical realm. The ultimate heaven will be heaven on earth.

Typically, we think of heaven as us leaving our place and going to be with God in His place. But from the Bible, we understand that the ultimate heaven will be where God leaves His place and comes to be with us in our place.

God will permanently reign on earth.

Satan will be eternally judged and removed from earth.

There will be no more sin.

The Lord's Prayer will be dramatically answered: "Your kingdom come, your will be done, on earth as it is in heaven."

God's people will live in resurrected bodies, on a resurrected earth, in a resurrected city – the New Jerusalem - serving a resurrected Lord.

In summary, the New Testament's emphasis regarding God's ultimate plan for mankind isn't on us going to heaven when we die, instead, the emphasis is on our resurrection and us experiencing a fully human (spirit, soul and body) eternal existence with God.

Two great books written on this subject are: "Heaven", by Randy Alcorn, and "Surprised by Hope", by Tom Wright.

WHAT DOES THE BIBLE SAY ABOUT SEX OUTSIDE OF MARRIAGE?

In our previous study, we learned that God calls us all to repent of our sins. True repentance that brings salvation will mean that we actively renounce and walk away from sinful behaviours. For each of us, this is a costly but necessary step. Making Jesus as Lord of our lives means prioritising our relationship with Him over our relationship with people and over our sexual desires and preferences.

"Anyone who loves their life will lose it, while anyone who hates their life in this world will keep it for eternal life." (John 12:25, NIV)

To understand why certain sexual practices are sinful we must go back to the beginning to see God's original design for human flourishing. In Genesis, God creates men and women and establishes the sacred institution of marriage—a union between one man and one woman for life. Jesus reaffirms this divine design in the New Testament as the timeless blueprint for humanity. The Bible consistently celebrates sex within marriage as good, life-giving, and to be enjoyed regularly. Conversely, any form of sexual activity outside this God-ordained marital bond is unequivocally condemned in the Bible. Sexual activity outside of marriage is not just considered a sin but is also detrimental to human flourishing.

Growing up in my house we had a real fire in the living room. We enjoyed the warmth it gave out, and the smell and crackle of burning wood. In the context of the hearth, the fire is a comforting thing. However, if you were to take the fire out of the hearth and set it loose in the living room, that same fire would become dangerous and destructive. Similarly, sex in the context of biblical marriage is wonderful and fulfilling, but outside this context, it can be immensely damaging and spiritually devastating.

In his first letter to the church in Corinth, Paul warns against sexual behaviour outside of the context of marriage:

"Or do you not know that the unrighteous will not inherit the kingdom of God? Do not be deceived: neither the sexually immoral ... nor adulterers, nor men who practice homosexuality ..." (1 Corinthians 6:9, ESV)

To be clear God's word isn't condemning our desires or temptations. We all have desires and we all face temptations. It is acting on these desires that the Bible is condemning.

Here Paul explicitly lists three sexual practices which are to be considered sinful, each of these practices is outside of the context of biblical marriage (i.e., one man and one woman for life):

- Sexual immorality: means every kind of sex outside of marriage, an obvious example is having sex before a couple get married.
- Adultery: meaning sex when either or both parties are already married.
- Homosexuality: sex between people of the same sex (see also Romans 1:26-27), i.e., outside of God's design from marriage.

So, the Bible is clear, if we are followers of Jesus, any sexual activity outside of the context of a God-ordained marriage is sinful and therefore to be repented of. Paul goes on to say:

"And such were some of you. But you were washed, you were sanctified, you were justified in the name of the Lord Jesus Christ and by the Spirit of our God." (1 Corinthians 6:11, ESV)

Repentance doesn't mean that we will never again struggle with sinful desires or temptation. Indeed, the struggle against sin will be a lifelong struggle, as we seek to honour God. Neither does it mean that we will never sin again. It means that with God's help, we are choosing to no longer pursue or justify a life of sin, but instead, we are seeking to live God's way.

I WAS CHRISTENED AS A CHILD. SHOULD I NOW BE BAPTISED AS A BELIEVER?

It is common in traditional Christian backgrounds for parents to have their newborn children 'baptised' or 'christened'. This would be a moment for the parents to publicly commit to raising their child in the Christian faith. In itself, this is a great thing. For some parents, christening is merely a religious tradition to be followed, but for others, it is a sincere expression of their genuine faith.

The problem with christening is that it isn't in the Bible!

There are 31 examples in the New Testament of people being baptised. On every occasion, baptism was a person's own decision in response to their personal faith, not that of their parents.

While Christening isn't in the Bible, we do see parents 'dedicating' their children to the Lord (see 1 Samuel 1:27-28, Mark 10:13-16). A child dedication service in church is a wonderful moment to celebrate a child's life, to pray a blessing on them and for the parents to commit to raising them in God's ways (see Proverbs 22:6).

The Bible doesn't teach infant baptism or adult baptism, it teaches believers' baptism. So, whether you have been christened as a child or not, God's word tells you to be baptised immediately after you put your faith in Jesus and turn from your sins.

AS A BELIEVER, I WAS SPRINKLED WITH WATER. SHOULD I NOW BE BAPTISED BY FULL IMMERSION?

The short answer is - yes!

In some Christian traditions, adult believers are 'sprinkled' with water in the name of the Father, Son and Holy Spirit. This sprinkling is referred to as a 'baptism'. For many people, this moment was highly significant in their faith journey. While this ceremony may have been an expression of a person's legitimate faith, was it a legitimate (i.e., biblical) baptism?

In our study, we discovered that the word for 'baptism' in Greek literally means 'to immerse' or 'to submerge'. It doesn't mean 'to sprinkle'. So, when the apostle Peter said, "Repent and be baptised" (Acts 2:38), he was instructing new believers to repent and be submerged in water. After Philip baptised the Ethiopian eunuch in Acts 8, we read that they "came up out of the water". The only type of baptism described in the Bible is by full immersion.

In Acts 19:1-6, Paul re-baptised a group of twelve believers. He did this not because their faith in Jesus was deficient, but because their baptism experience was incomplete. It is very important, then, that each of us is properly baptised.

Just as we want you to have real faith and real repentance, we encourage you to have a real baptism experience by being fully immersed in water.

I WAS BAPTISED YEARS AGO BUT SINCE THEN FELL AWAY. NOW THAT I'VE COME BACK TO GOD, DO I NEED TO BE BAPTISED AGAIN?

If you were baptised properly in the first place, namely, as a believer and by full immersion, then you do not need to be baptised again. Baptism is a foundation, which once laid doesn't need to be repeated.

Jesus, anticipating that Peter would fall away, said to him: "I have prayed for you, Simon, that your faith may not fail. And when you have turned back, strengthen your brothers." (Luke 22:32, NIV) Jesus did not require Peter to be baptised again, but He did expect him to turn back and repent. Baptism only happens once, but repentance will happen many times in our lives.

MY PARENTS DON'T WANT ME TO BE BAPTISED. SHOULD I OBEY THE BIBLE OR MY PARENTS?

The Bible teaches that children should obey their parents (see Ephesians 6:1). As a child grows into adulthood, they shift from having to obey their parents to having to honour them. The word 'to honour' in Hebrew means 'to make heavy'. So, we should always give weight to our parents' opinions.

That said, Jesus taught: "Anyone who loves their father or mother more than me is not worthy of me …" (Matthew 10:37, NIV). This means that our primary allegiance is to God first, above our parents. As adult believers, we are to obey God in getting baptised, even if it goes against the wishes of our parents. But we should seek to honour our parents in the way we go about this, with respect, with dialogue and with love.

If a child becomes a Christian and their parents do not consent to them being baptised, in this case, it would be right for them to obey their parents and wait. They should wait until their parents change their minds or until they are of an age to make their own decision as an adult.

WHERE I LIVE, CHRISTIANS ARE PERSECUTED. SHOULD I RISK GETTING PUBLICLY BAPTISED?

In many parts of the world where Christians are persecuted, being baptised publicly is very risky. In such environments, we would encourage baptisms to happen privately.

STUDY 3
BAPTISM WITH THE HOLY SPIRIT

If you wanted to come to my house and need directions, there are a couple of ways I could help you. Firstly, I could give you a map and hope that your map-reading skills are good enough to find your way. Another option would be to provide you with a map and also my presence – I would get in the car with you and guide you the whole way. The second option is guaranteed to get you to my house.

God has a specific plan for His church and your life. Thankfully in this journey of life, He doesn't leave us to struggle through by ourselves. Instead, God has provided us with His word - the Bible, which is like a map for us. He has also provided us with His presence in our lives. With both the word of God and the Spirit of God we can navigate our way into His purpose.

In this study, we are going to look at the gift of the Holy Spirit, which God has given to believers.

In the first study, we affirmed our belief in the Trinity, that God has eternally existed in three Persons - Father, Son and Holy Spirit. As we now go on to study in more detail the work of the Holy Spirit in our lives, we must remember that the Spirit is not an impersonal force or an atmosphere - He's God Himself. The Holy Spirit is God's very presence dwelling in our lives (see John 14:23, 1 Corinthians 3:16).

In the previous study, we looked at our response to the gospel, namely that we are to believe in Jesus, repent for our sins and be baptised in water. We also learned that God responds to us as believers by giving us the gift of the Holy Spirit as a sign that we are now securely His. God gives us His Spirit at the moment of our salvation, the moment we turn to Him in faith (see Ephesians 4:30, Romans 8:9).

> "In Him, you also, after listening to the message of truth, the gospel of your salvation - having also believed, you were sealed in Him with the Holy Spirit of the promise ..." (Ephesians 1:13, NASB)

While we receive the Holy Spirit upon conversion, we discover in the pages of Acts that there is another experience that God gives to His people, called the baptism with the Holy Spirit. From scripture, we see that this experience was typically separate from and subsequent to a person's conversion.

Let's go on a journey through Acts to discover how God blesses His people so that we can also experience this great baptism with the Holy Spirit in our lives.

JESUS' FINAL INSTRUCTIONS (ACTS 1)

Following His resurrection, Jesus instructed the disciples:

> "Do not leave Jerusalem, but wait for the gift my Father promised, which you have heard me speak about. For John baptised with water, but in a few days you will be baptised with the Holy Spirit ... you will receive power when the Holy Spirit comes on you; and you will be my witnesses in Jerusalem, and in all Judea and Samaria, and to the ends of the earth." (Acts 1:4-5, 8, NIV)

As eyewitnesses of Jesus' death and resurrection, the disciples were bursting with passion to tell the world all about Him. Their message was so compelling, their testimony so powerful and authentic, that nothing or no one could stop them. However, even with all this, the disciples needed to wait for the Holy Spirit's power before they could witness. To change the world, we need more than clever arguments, dramatic testimonies and skilful communication - we need the power of the Holy Spirit. Only He can change a life, only He can convict and convert.

You can't accomplish God's plan without God's power. But with the power of the Holy Spirit, we can see results greater than would be humanly possible. Partnering with the Holy Spirit is the secret of a successful church and a successful life. The book of Acts serves as a stunning example of how God can accomplish extraordinary things through ordinary people who are led by the Holy Spirit. The full title of the book of Acts is 'The Acts of the Apostles'. An alternative title could be 'The Acts of the Holy Spirit through the apostles and ordinary believers'.

> "Now to Him who is able to carry out His purpose and do superabundantly more than all that we dare ask or think infinitely beyond our greatest prayers, hopes, or dreams, according to His power that is at work within us ..." (Ephesians 3:20, AMP)

We previously learned that the word 'baptise' in Greek ("baptizō") means to immerse. Here Jesus is telling the disciples, and us, to expect an experience of immersion in the Holy Spirit. Elsewhere in Acts, this experience is described in a variety of different ways:

> "All of them were **filled** with the Holy Spirit..." (Acts 2:4, NIV)

> "... the Holy Spirit **came on them** as he had come on us at the beginning." (Acts 11:15, NIV)

> "...they prayed for the new believers there that they might **receive** the Holy Spirit ..." (Acts 8:15, NIV)

Therefore, to be baptised with the Holy Spirit is also to be filled, to have the Holy Spirit come upon you and to receive the Holy Spirit. To illustrate this experience imagine submerging a dry sponge in a bucket of water. You could say it has been immersed – or baptized - but at the same time you could also say it received the water into itself, that indeed it is filled with the water and the water came upon it.

This illustration is also helpful in describing what happens after we are baptised with the Holy Spirit. When the sponge is lifted out of the bucket, the water continues to drip from it soaking anything it touches. We come to God like dry sponges, thirsty for His presence. Having been filled with His Spirit, we now overflow with blessings that touch the lives of those around us.

> "Jesus said: 'Let anyone who is thirsty come to me and drink. Whoever believes in me, as Scripture has said, rivers of living water will flow from within them.' By this he meant the Spirit, whom those who believed in him were later to receive." (John 7:37-39, NIV)

Acts chapter 1 records that there were 120 believers including the apostles who were waiting and praying in anticipation of the Holy Spirit. On the day of Pentecost, the Holy Spirit came, just as Jesus promised. Starting with Pentecost we will now study the five instances of baptism with the Holy Spirit recorded in Acts. We believe that God has deliberately provided these five examples to show us what we can expect to happen in our lives.

1ST EXAMPLE: THE DAY OF PENTECOST (ACTS 2)

> "When the day of Pentecost had come, they were all together in one place. And suddenly a noise like a violent rushing wind came from heaven, and it filled the whole house where they were sitting. And tongues that looked like fire appeared to them, distributing themselves, and a tongue rested on each one of them. And they were all filled with the Holy Spirit and began to speak with different tongues, as the Spirit was giving them the ability to speak out. Now there were Jews residing in Jerusalem, devout men from every nation under heaven. And when this sound occurred, the crowd came together and they were bewildered, because each one of them was hearing them speak in his own language. They were amazed and astonished, saying, "Why, are not all these who are speaking Galileans? And how is it that we each hear them in our own language to which we were born? Parthians, Medes, and Elamites, and residents of Mesopotamia, Judea, and Cappadocia, Pontus and Asia,

Phrygia and Pamphylia, Egypt and the parts of Libya around Cyrene, and visitors from Rome, both Jews and proselytes, Cretans and Arabs—we hear them speaking in our own tongues of the mighty deeds of God." And they all continued in amazement and great perplexity, saying to one another, "What does this mean?" But others were jeering and saying, "They are full of sweet wine!" But Peter, taking his stand with the other eleven, raised his voice and declared to them: "Men of Judea and all you who live in Jerusalem, know this, and pay attention to my words. For these people are not drunk, as you assume, since it is only the third hour of the day; but this is what has been spoken through the prophet Joel: 'And it shall be in the last days,' God says, 'That I will pour out My Spirit on all mankind ...'" (Acts 2:1-17, NASB)

God deliberately chose to pour out His Spirit on the day of Pentecost. The day of Pentecost had agricultural significance, marking the beginning of the wheat harvest. The outpouring of the Holy Spirit and the birth of the church 2000 years ago was the beginning of the global harvest of souls coming to Christ. It is a harvest that will culminate with a multitude that no one can number:

"I looked, and behold, a great multitude that no one could number, from every nation, from all tribes and peoples and languages, standing before the throne and before the Lamb, clothed in white robes ..." (Revelation 7:9, ESV)

The book of Acts chronicles the stunning growth of the church in the first 30 years of its existence. Indeed, as we look at the past 2000 years, we see how the mighty Holy Spirit has caused His church to emerge and grow. Today, one in seven people are part of the Church! According to research by Ralph Winter, founder of the US Center for Missions (now Frontier Ventures), the ratio of non-believers to believers has steadily declined over the centuries, as the following illustration shows.

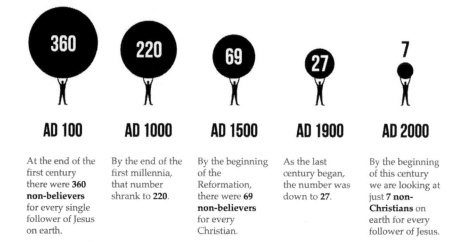

AD 100

At the end of the first century there were **360 non-believers** for every single follower of Jesus on earth.

AD 1000

By the end of the first millennia, that number shrank to **220**.

AD 1500

By the beginning of the Reformation, there were **69 non-believers** for every Christian.

AD 1900

As the last century began, the number was down to **27**.

AD 2000

By the beginning of this century we are looking at just **7 non-Christians** on earth for every follower of Jesus.

In the past century, the Pentecostal/Charismatic movement is a modern testament to how the Holy Spirit can grow the church and transform the world by working through His people. The movement began in 1906 in Los Angeles, where William Seymour, a one-eyed, 34-year-old, son of African slaves, started a prayer meeting. The prayer meeting was in a small house on a street called North Bonnie Brae. They experienced an outpouring of the Holy Spirit just as the early believers did in Acts chapter 2. The prayer meeting then continued over days and weeks. Large numbers started to gather. To create space for the crowds wanting to come, they relocated their gathering and rented a small timber-clad building on Azusa Street. The meetings grew in size with 800 people crammed inside and an overflow of 500 people standing outside listening. They would go on to have several meetings each day and the revival lasted for years. There were countless testimonies of people experiencing the gift of tongues, and other gifts of the Holy Spirit and many dramatic miracles were recorded.

One hundred years on from the Azusa Street revival, the impact of this movement is staggering:

> Today there are 700 million Pentecostal/charismatic Christians [That's nearly one in ten people on earth!]. (Allan Anderson's "Global

Pentecostalism," a paper presented at the Wheaton Theology Conference, 2015)

Pentecostal churches globally are growing at a rate of 35,000 new people a day. It's estimated that globally Pentecostalism will exceed 800 million adherents by 2025. ("The Pentecostal Renewal," World Christian Encyclopedia)

On Pentecost, we note that two supernatural signs accompanied the coming of the Holy Spirit. Firstly, we read that "a violent rushing wind came from heaven..." (Acts 2:2). The word for "Spirit" in the Hebrew Old Testament was "Rûach" and in the Greek New Testament the word was "Pneuma". Both translate to 'wind' or 'breath'. It seems appropriate that the coming of the Holy Spirit, be signified by a "violent rushing wind."

In 1995, a revival started in a church in Brownsville, Pensacola (Florida). John Kilpatrick recalls the moment in a church meeting when the revival started: "Suddenly, I felt a wind blow through my legs, just like in the second chapter of the Book of Acts. Both of my ankles flipped over so that I could hardly stand."

The other sign was the fire. We read: "And tongues that looked like fire appeared to them ..." (Acts 2:3). Throughout scripture, fire is used to signify God's presence - the burning bush, the pillar of fire and fire on Sinai. The message of Pentecost was clear: God is now present among His people.

In the Old Testament, God put His Spirit on the select few - kings, prophets and judges. But here in the New Testament, we now see God pouring out His Spirit on all mankind! We read that "they were all filled with the Holy Spirit." In fact, the Bible describes us as special places for the Holy Spirit to dwell.

"Do you not know that your bodies are temples of the Holy Spirit, who is in you, whom you have received from God?" (1 Corinthians 6:19, NIV)

In the Old Testament, God had a temple for His people, but in the New Testament God has a people for His temple. God dwells among us - what a privilege!

On the day of Pentecost, the Bible records that 3,000 people became believers and were baptised (see Acts 2:41). The chapters that follow record how the church in Jerusalem grew exponentially. By Acts 4, the number of men in the church was 5,000. Include women and children and this would have been a five-figure congregation. It is therefore no surprise that the Jewish authorities unleased a wave of persecution against the church in Jerusalem, beginning with the killing of the first martyr Stephen.

> "And Saul approved of their killing him [Stephen]. On that day a great persecution broke out against the church in Jerusalem, and all except the apostles were scattered throughout Judea and Samaria." (Acts 8:1, NIV)

Amazingly, God used this persecution to actually spread the message into the surrounding regions (see Acts 1:8) and grow the church. This leads us to the next example of people being baptised with the Holy Spirit.

2ND EXAMPLE: THE BELIEVERS IN SAMARIA (ACTS 8)

> "Those who had been scattered preached the word wherever they went. Philip went down to a city in Samaria and proclaimed the Messiah there. When the crowds heard Philip and saw the signs he performed, they all paid close attention to what he said. For with shrieks, impure spirits came out of many, and many who were paralysed or lame were healed. So, there was great joy in that city. Now for some time a man named Simon had practised sorcery in the city and amazed all the people of Samaria. He boasted that he was someone great, and all the people, both high and low, gave him their attention and exclaimed, "This man is rightly called the Great Power of God." They followed him because he had amazed them for a long time with his sorcery. But when they believed Philip as he proclaimed the good news of the kingdom of God

and the name of Jesus Christ, they were baptised, both men and women. Simon himself believed and was baptised. And he followed Philip everywhere, astonished by the great signs and miracles he saw. When the apostles in Jerusalem heard that Samaria had accepted the word of God, they sent Peter and John to Samaria. When they arrived, they prayed for the new believers there that they might receive the Holy Spirit, because the Holy Spirit had not yet come on any of them; they had simply been baptised in the name of the Lord Jesus. Then Peter and John placed their hands on them, and they received the Holy Spirit. When Simon saw that the Spirit was given at the laying on of the apostles' hands, he offered them money and said, "Give me also this ability so that everyone on whom I lay my hands may receive the Holy Spirit." Peter answered: "May your money perish with you, because you thought you could buy the gift of God with money!" (Acts 8:4-20, NIV)

From these verses, it is clear that the baptism with the Holy Spirit is a separate and subsequent experience to a person's conversion. These were authentic believers, who had been baptised in water, yet "the Holy Spirit had not yet come on any of them."

Acts chapter 8 does not say if those experiencing the Holy Spirit spoke in tongues, however it does allude to them having some form of observable and impressive experience: "When Simon saw that the Spirit was given at the laying on of the apostles' hands, he offered them money and said, 'Give me also this ability …'" What did he see that excited him so much? This experience would likely have followed a similar pattern to Acts chapter 2 and the other examples in Acts which included people speaking in tongues.

3ᴿᴰ EXAMPLE: ANANIAS PRAYS WITH SAUL (ACTS 9)

The persecution of the church was being driven by a young zealous Jew named Saul. In Acts chapter 9 we read of his dramatic conversion experience.

"Saul was still breathing out murderous threats against the Lord's disciples. He went to the high priest and asked him for letters to the synagogues in Damascus, so that if he found any there who belonged to the Way, whether men or women, he might take them as prisoners to Jerusalem. As he neared Damascus on his journey, suddenly a light from heaven flashed around him. He fell to the ground and heard a voice say to him, "Saul, Saul, why do you persecute me?" "Who are you, Lord?" Saul asked. "I am Jesus, whom you are persecuting," he replied. "Now get up and go into the city, and you will be told what you must do." The men travelling with Saul stood there speechless; they heard the sound but did not see anyone. Saul got up from the ground, but when he opened his eyes, he could see nothing. So, they led him by hand into Damascus. For three days he was blind and did not eat or drink anything. In Damascus there was a disciple named Ananias. The Lord called to him in a vision, "Ananias!" "Yes, Lord," he answered. The Lord told him, "Go to the house of Judas on Straight Street and ask for a man from Tarsus named Saul, for he is praying... Then Ananias went to the house and entered it. Placing his hands on Saul, he said, "Brother Saul, the Lord - Jesus, who appeared to you on the road as you were coming here - has sent me so that you may see again and be filled with the Holy Spirit." Immediately, something like scales fell from Saul's eyes, and he could see again. He got up and was baptised ..." (Acts 9:1-11, 17-18, NIV)

Saul's life was turned around. He went from being one of the greatest persecutors of the church to being one of the greatest propagators of the church. He went from being the persecutor to being the persecuted. He went from being called Saul to changing his name to Paul. And he went on to write much of the New Testament!

Ananias prayed for Saul to "be filled with the Holy Spirit," but the verses don't unpack for us what happened in that moment. Did he speak in tongues? Did he prophesy? We can't say for sure, however, years later, Paul describing his own prayer life says: "I thank God that I speak in tongues more than all of you." (1 Corinthians 14:18, NIV). Based on the other examples in Acts, it would seem likely that this gift first came after being prayed for by Ananias.

4ᵀᴴ EXAMPLE: PETER AT CORNELIUS' HOUSE (ACTS 10)

Acts chapter 10 is a pivotal moment for the early church. Up to this point, the believers were from Jewish backgrounds. However, in Acts 10, we see God opening the door into the Gentile (non-Jewish) world. The chapter describes how God led the apostle Peter to a Roman centurion named Cornelius, in a town called Caesarea. When Peter and his companions arrive, they are ushered into a "large gathering of people" in the centurion's house. Peter then proceeds to share the gospel with those present:

> "While Peter was still speaking these words, the Holy Spirit came on all who heard the message. The circumcised believers who had come with Peter were astonished that the gift of the Holy Spirit had been poured out even on Gentiles. For they heard them speaking in tongues and praising God. Then Peter said, "Surely no one can stand in the way of their being baptised with water. They have received the Holy Spirit just as we have." So, he ordered that they be baptised in the name of Jesus Christ. Then they asked Peter to stay with them for a few days." (Acts 10:44-48, NIV)

The Holy Spirit interrupted Peter's message and filled all those present! For Peter and his companions, the evidence that the Gentiles were baptised with the Holy Spirit was that "they heard them speaking in tongues and praising God". Just like the sponge, the water pouring out is evidence that it has been immersed. When a person is filled with the Spirit, you can fully expect them to overflow with praise and spiritual words.

It is also worth noting the importance and the weight that Peter places on water baptism. This links back to our last study. We read: "So he ordered that they be baptised in the name of Jesus Christ." Cornelius and his friends were clearly saved, evidenced by the fact that God baptised them with His Spirit (see Acts 15:8). Being baptised was not essential for their salvation, but it was essential for their obedience and to walk free from the past. It is the same for us.

5TH EXAMPLE: THE DISCIPLES IN EPHESUS (ACTS 19)

> "… Paul took the road through the interior and arrived at Ephesus. There he found some disciples and asked them, "Did you receive the Holy Spirit when you believed?" They answered, "No, we have not even heard that there is a Holy Spirit." So, Paul asked, "Then what baptism did you receive?" "John's baptism," they replied. Paul said, "John's baptism was a baptism of repentance. He told the people to believe in the one coming after him, that is, in Jesus." On hearing this, they were baptised in the name of the Lord Jesus. When Paul placed his hands on them, the Holy Spirit came on them, and they spoke in tongues and prophesied." (Acts 19:1-6, NIV)

In this final example, we see Paul in the early stages of planting the church in Ephesus, a church which became one of the largest churches on earth at the time.

In conversation with some new believers, Paul opens with the question: "Did you receive the Holy Spirit when you believed?" Again, it is evident from this question that being baptised with the Holy Spirit typically happens separately from your conversion.

Note that the believers both "spoke in tongues and prophesied". The gift of tongues is someone, inspired by the Holy Spirit, speaking in a foreign language; prophecy is someone's inspired words in their own language. The baptism with the Holy Spirit will result in an overflow of words. As Jesus said: "… rivers of living water will flow from within them." By this he meant the Spirit, whom those who believed in him were later to receive." (John 7:38-39, NIV)

SUMMARY OF THE 5 EXAMPLES

To fully understand God's pattern and to know what to expect when a person is baptised with the Holy Spirit, it is helpful to ask a series of questions for each of the five examples in Acts:

	Acts 2	Acts 8	Acts 9	Acts 10	Acts 19
Were they already Christians?	Yes	Yes	Yes	Yes (only just)	Yes
Was this experience before or after their water baptism?	After	After	Before	Before	After
Did they speak in tongues?	Yes	Doesn't say	Doesn't say	Yes	Yes
Were there other supernatural manifestations?	Yes (wind and fire)	Yes (Simon saw)	Yes (scales)	Yes (praise)	Yes (prophecy)
Did someone lay hands on them?	No	Yes	Yes	No	Yes

5 CONCLUSIONS FROM THE 5 EXAMPLES

- The baptism with the Spirit is for every believer and typically happens separately from their conversion.
- The order you are baptised in isn't important. What is important is that you experience both water baptism and baptism with the Holy Spirit.
- You can expect to speak in tongues when you are baptised with the Holy Spirit. In three of the five examples, it explicitly states that they spoke in tongues. The other two examples do not clearly state that they spoke in tongues, but the wider passage suggests that it may have happened. Bible teacher, George Alexander, puts it very well in his book, 'Into Liberty': "If we ask, 'Must I speak in tongues?' the answer is no. But it's better to ask the question, 'May I speak in tongues?' And the answer to that question is apparently yes." (George Alexander, "Into Liberty," p31)
- When you are baptised with the Holy Spirit, you can also expect to see other supernatural manifestations, such as spontaneous praise or prophecy. In our experience, it's also common for people to shake, fall down or even be overcome with joy.

- While God can just fill you with His Spirit – He is the sovereign God after all - we also see from Acts that it was normal for someone to pray over you to receive this experience.

HOW TO RECEIVE THE BAPTISM WITH THE HOLY SPIRIT

1 Believe the promise

God has promised to pour out His Holy Spirit. Believe that His promise is for you today.

> "'And it shall be in the last days,' God says, 'That I will pour out My Spirit on all mankind ...'" (Acts 2:17, NASB)

2 Ask the Father

> Jesus said: "Which of you fathers, if your son asks for a fish, will give him a snake instead? Or if he asks for an egg, will give him a scorpion? If you then, though you are evil, know how to give good gifts to your children, how much more will your Father in heaven give the Holy Spirit to those who ask him!" (Luke 11:11-13, NIV)

When you ask God for His Spirit, that is what you will receive. It seems God typically will not force anything upon us. Instead, He works with our free will and waits to be asked. Indeed, we are not just to ask, but we ask with a deep spiritual thirst. As Jesus said: "Let anyone who is thirsty come to me and drink."

3 Ask someone to pray for you

Ask someone to pray for you and lay hands on you. This could be in a church gathering, a small group gathering, at your house or in a quiet outdoor setting.

4 Receive the Holy Spirit and expect to speak in tongues

Having asked for the Spirit, now we are to receive the Spirit by faith. Wait expectantly in His presence, focus on Him by worshipping, and in this atmosphere of expectation and worship you will receive.

Just like in Acts, you can expect to speak in tongues having received the Holy Spirit. Often it will happen straight away, sometimes it happens afterwards.

When we speak in our native language the words come from our brain. However, when we speak in tongues, the language comes from our hearts, not our heads (see 1 Corinthians 14:14). Just as Jesus described it: "… rivers of living water will flow from within them."

It is important to remember that God will not force you to speak in tongues. Scripture says that they "began to speak with different tongues, as the Spirit was giving them the ability …" (Acts 2:4, NASB). The Holy Spirit will give you the ability and the words, but you have to speak.

5 Keep being filled

We are encouraged in scripture to: "… be filled with the Holy Spirit …" (Ephesians 5:18). "Be filled" in the Greek more accurately translates "be being filled." Being filled with the Spirit is to be an ongoing experience in our lives, like standing in a river that's continuously flowing. Indeed, we see the early disciples being continually filled as they came back to God asking for His strength (see Acts 4:31).

The greatest part of this experience isn't the ability to speak in tongues - it's the fact that God Himself comes close to us. So, remember, don't chase an experience; rather pursue and love God.

FREQUENTLY ASKED QUESTIONS

I WAS PRAYED FOR BUT DID NOT EXPERIENCE BEING FILLED WITH THE HOLY SPIRIT. WHAT SHOULD I DO?

Everyone's experience of being filled with the Holy Spirit is different. For some, being filled with the Spirit is dramatic, for others, it's less so. For some, it is an immediate experience, while for others it happens after a period of patiently seeking God. Some describe physical sensations, such as shaking, heat, power surging through them or joy and laughter. But others have no physical indicators, just a wonderful peace.

Some people wrongly conclude that they did not receive the Holy Spirit because their experience was not as dramatic as someone else's.

While our experiences are highly subjective, the Bible gives us two objective indicators that we've been filled. We should expect to see both the gifts (see Study 6) and fruits (see Galatians 5:22-23) of the Holy Spirit starting to operate in our lives.

If you are unsure you have been filled with the Holy Spirit, simply ask again. In Matthew 7:7 Jesus said: "Ask and it will be given to you …" The Amplified translation gives us a fuller take on this verse: "Ask and **keep on asking** and it will be given to you …"

HOW DO I KNOW IF I AM TRULY SPEAKING IN TONGUES OR JUST MAKING IT UP?

It is not uncommon for people to doubt their personal experience of speaking in tongues. While it is possible that they are just making up a language (although this is not as easy as you'd think), more often the doubts come from a confusion of what is actually happening when they speak.

Our normal experience of speaking, since childhood, involves us thinking and then speaking. But speaking in tongues is different. When someone speaks in tongues, the language comes from their "innermost being" (John 7:38). They are speaking from their heart, not their head. Paul described it this way: "… if I pray in a tongue, my spirit prays, but my mind is unfruitful." (1 Corinthians 14:14, NIV)

Scientific research has confirmed what the Bible describes. In 2006, the New York Times published an article entitled: "A Neuroscientific Look at Speaking in Tongues." They reported: "Researchers at the University of Pennsylvania took brain images of five women while they spoke in tongues and found that their frontal lobes — the thinking, willful part of the brain through which people control what they do — were relatively quiet, as were the language centers. The regions involved in maintaining self-consciousness were active." Further, they reported: "A recent study of nearly 1,000 evangelical Christians in England found that those who engaged in the practice [of speaking in tongues] were more emotionally stable than those who did not."

It would be wrong to allow your doubts to stop you from using this wonderful gift from God. Instead of over-analysing what's coming out of your mouth, simply focus on God. Express your love for Him in your language or your new language (1 Corinthians 13:1, 14:15). As you do this, you will grow stronger on the inside and be built up in your faith (Jude 1:20, 1 Corinthians 14:4).

IN SOME CHRISTIAN CIRCLES, THEY TEACH THAT THE GIFTS OF THE HOLY SPIRIT CEASED ONCE THE BIBLE WAS COMPLETED AND THE FIRST GENERATION OF APOSTLES PASSED AWAY. HOW DO WE KNOW THAT THESE GIFTS ARE STILL AVAILABLE TODAY?

The belief that the gifts of the Spirit have passed away is called cessationism. Cessationism comes from a legitimate concern, yet it is based on a bad interpretation of scripture.

Cessationist concern is that if we believe the gift of prophecy is still operating today, what would stop someone from claiming that their word from God should be given the same weight as The Word of God, i.e., the Bible. This is a fair concern. While scripture is to be wholeheartedly believed and obeyed, prophecies are to be weighed before being embraced. This was encouraged by Paul in his first letter to the Corinthians: "Two or three prophets should speak, and the others should weigh carefully what is said." (1 Corinthians 14:29, NIV) By what standard should all prophecies be judged? It is by the Bible. If someone is prophesying by the power of the Spirit, it will always align with, and never contradict, the scriptures that the same Holy Spirit inspired. We are fallible and can make mistakes, but God and His word, the Bible, are infallible.

Cessationism is based on a wrong interpretation of 1 Corinthians 13:

> "Love never fails; but if there are gifts of prophecy, they will be done away; if there are tongues, they will cease; if there is knowledge, it will be done away. For we know in part and we prophesy in part; but when the perfect comes, the partial will be done away. When I was a child, I used to speak like a child, think like a child, reason like a child; when I became a man, I did away with childish things. For now we see in a mirror dimly, but then face to face; now I know in part, but then I will know fully just as I also have been fully known." (1 Corinthians 13:8-12, NASB)

From these verses, cessationists would teach that the gifts of the Holy Spirit passed away when "the perfect comes," which they believe was the completion of the Bible in its final form. They would teach that there is no longer any need for prophecies because we now have everything that God wants to say written in scripture. This whole teaching is based on their wrong assumption of what "when the perfect comes" means.

In our first study, we talked about using good hermeneutics when interpreting the Bible. Here are two of the principles we mentioned:

- Read the text in its context
- Understand the unclear in the light of the clear

To understand what "when the perfect comes" means, we must look at its immediate context. Paul used other phrases to make the same point. He said: "For now we see in a mirror dimly, but then face to face; now I know in part, but then I will know fully just as I also have been fully known." It is apparent from the immediate context that "the perfect" refers to the moment when we will all see Him "face to face" and "will know fully just as I also have been fully known". These phrases point not to the completion of the Bible, but rather to our ultimate face-to-face meeting with Jesus at His return. This is also confirmed as you look at the broader context of the whole Bible. We understand that the gifts of the Holy Spirit will continue to be given until Jesus returns. In Acts 2 we read:

> "... it shall be in the last days,' God says, 'That I will pour forth of My Spirit on all mankind; and your sons and your daughters shall prophesy, and your young men shall see visions, and your old men shall dream dreams; even on My bondslaves, both men and women, I will in those days pour forth of My Spirit and they shall prophesy. ... Before the great and glorious day of the Lord shall come." (Acts 2:17-18, 20, NASB)

Also in Ephesians 4, we learn that the ministry gifts of apostle, prophet, evangelist, pastor and teacher will be continually given to the church "until" the church becomes a place of great maturity and Christ-like stature.

> "He gave some as apostles, and some as prophets, and some as evangelists, and some as pastors and teachers, for the equipping of the

saints for the work of service, to the building up of the body of Christ; until we all attain to the unity of the faith, and of the knowledge of the Son of God, to a mature man, to the measure of the stature which belongs to the fullness of Christ." (Ephesians 4:11-13, NASB)

These verses in Ephesians again point to a great future moment when Jesus will return for His prepared church. As it says in Revelation: "… the marriage of the Lamb has come and His bride has made herself ready." (Revelation 19:7, NASB)

The New Testament is full of examples, clear instructions and encouragements relating to the gifts of the Holy Spirit. In light of this, it would seem strange that they are no longer around today because of one slightly ambiguous verse in 1 Corinthians 13. The natural flow and reading of the text do not lead to a cessationist view. Jack Deere, in his book 'Surprised by the Power of the Spirit', puts it well:

"If you were to lock a brand-new Christian in a room with a Bible and tell him to study what the Scriptures have to say about healing and miracles, he would never come out of the room a cessationist."

In summary, we believe that Paul in 1 Corinthians 13 is teaching us that the gifts of the Holy Spirit will eventually be "done away" with when we see Jesus "face to face" at His second coming. Indeed, the gifts of the Spirit and the ministry gifts are given to prepare us, His Bride, to be ready and mature in advance of that "great and glorious day of the Lord". In our generation, more than ever, we need to see these great gifts operating.

HOW DO I KNOW THAT THE TONGUES I SPEAK IN ARE NOT COUNTERFEIT?

In the Bible, we see examples of Satan producing counterfeit versions of the good gifts that God gives. For example, we see true teachers and false teachers, true prophets and false prophets, true apostles and false apostles. While the Bible does not explicitly refer to false tongues, it certainly would be consistent with the enemy's tactics that such a thing would exist. So how can you be sure that the gift of tongues you received is the real thing? Here is Jesus' answer to this concern:

> "Which of you fathers, if your son asks for a fish, will give him a snake instead? Or if he asks for an egg, will give him a scorpion? If you then, though you are evil, know how to give good gifts to your children, how much more will your Father in heaven give the Holy Spirit to those who ask him!" (Luke 11:11-13, NIV)

Jesus assures us if we ask the Father for the Holy Spirit, He's not going to give us a dangerous counterfeit, He can be trusted to give us the good gift of the Holy Spirit.

An important way of testing if a spiritual experience is from God or not is to look at where the focus is. The Holy Spirit has one clear agenda and ambition - to exalt Jesus. Paul wrote:

> "I want you to know that no one who is speaking by the Spirit of God says, 'Jesus be cursed,' and no one can say, 'Jesus is Lord,' except by the Holy Spirit." (1 Corinthians 12:3, NIV)

Jesus taught:

> "... the Spirit of truth who proceeds from the Father, He will testify about Me ..." (John 15:26, NASB)

And again, Jesus said concerning the Spirit:

> "He will glorify Me ..." (John 16:14, NASB)

The Bible teaches that the Holy Spirit has come to glorify Jesus. The Holy Spirit has not come to make you look good. He has not even come to make Himself look good. He came to make Jesus look good. Frank Bartleman, a key leader in the 1906 Azusa Street revival, said:

> "Any work that exalts the Holy Spirit or the gifts above Jesus will finally end up in fanaticism. Whatever causes us to exalt and love Jesus is well

and safe. The reverse will ruin all. The Holy Spirit is a great light but will always be focused on Jesus for His revealing."

The evidence that the Holy Spirit is working in our lives will be a greater love for Jesus and a passion to make Him known. That's how you know if the Holy Spirit is truly working in your life.

THE CHURCH AND GOD'S GLOBAL PLAN

As humans, we are prone to changing our plans. If Plan A doesn't work out, we move quickly to Plan B. Not so with God. He has had one plan since the beginning of time, and despite huge setbacks, His Plan A is on track. The very first chapter of the Bible sets it out for us, and the rest of scripture - indeed the rest of history – unpacks, unveils and implements it.

GOD'S COMMISSION TO MANKIND

In Genesis chapter 1, we read:

> "So God created human beings in his own image. In the image of God he created them; male and female he created them. Then God blessed them and said, 'Be fruitful and multiply. Fill the earth and govern it.'" (Genesis 1:27-28, NLT)

God's plan from the beginning has been to have a people who reflect His image, who fill the earth and usher in His Kingdom. As we'll discover as we go through this scripture, these people are none other than the Church!

In the beginning, our authority on earth came from the fact that we were under God's authority. However, two chapters later, in Genesis 3, we rejected God's rule and submitted to Satan. In doing so, we handed over our lives and this earth to the authority of this fallen angel (see Isaiah 14:12-15, Ezekiel 28:12-19). That is why thousands of years later, when Jesus was tempted by the devil in the wilderness, Satan claimed to have possession of all the kingdoms of the world:

> "... he led Him [Jesus] up and showed Him all the kingdoms of the world in a moment of time. And the devil said to Him, "I will give You all this domain and its glory; for it has been handed over to me, and I give it to whomever I wish." (Luke 4:5-6, NASB)

Indeed, the apostle John acknowledges that: "...the whole world lies in the power of the evil one." (1 John 5:19, ESV)

Despite this catastrophic setback, God did not abandon Plan A. He would have a people reflecting His glory, filling the earth and paving the way for His Kingdom. As we journey through the Bible, we see God working towards this great plan.

GOD'S PROMISE TO ABRAHAM

> "The LORD had said to Abram, 'Leave your country, your people and your father's household and go to the land I will show you. I will make you into a great nation and I will bless you; I will make your name great, and you will be a blessing. I will bless those who bless you, and whoever curses you I will curse; and all peoples on earth will be blessed through you.'" (Genesis 12:1-3, NIV)

God promised Abram - soon to be called Abraham - that from him, a great people would emerge and through this people, all nations would be blessed. How has God fulfilled this promise?

Firstly, God fulfilled this promise through Abram's offspring. Miraculously, Abraham and his wife Sarah in their old age had a son called Isaac, then Isaac had a son called Jacob (also called Israel) and

Israel had twelve sons, who in time formed the tribes of Israel. While the people of Israel have brought many blessings to the world, the main way "all peoples on earth" have been blessed by Israel is through one Israelite in particular - that is Jesus.

Jesus' atoning death and resurrection have brought salvation, forgiveness and blessing to all people.

But there's a third way God is fulfilling this great promise to Abraham. The Bible teaches that as believers we are Abraham's spiritual offspring:

"...if you belong to Christ, then you are Abraham's descendants, heirs according to promise." (Galatians 3:29, NASB)

Today, God is fulfilling His promise to Abraham through us, the church. God intends that blessing will come to all the nations, through the church filling the earth, sharing the life-giving message of Jesus, and ushering in His kingdom. We are God's Plan A!

"Then Jesus came to them and said, "All authority in heaven and on earth has been given to me. Therefore go and make disciples of all nations, baptising them in the name of the Father and of the Son and of the Holy Spirit, and teaching them to obey everything I have commanded you. And surely I am with you always, to the very end of the age." (Matthew 28:18-20, NIV)

GOD'S PROMISE TO DAVID

When the people of Israel had settled in the Promised Land, God raised up a great king called David. God gave this promise to him:

"When your days are over and you rest with your fathers, I will raise up your offspring to succeed you, who will come from your own body, and I will establish his kingdom. He is the one who will build a house for my Name, and I will establish the throne of his kingdom forever. I will be his father, and he will be my son." (2 Samuel 7:12-14, NIV)

Just as a camera can have a macro lens for close-up photos and a telephoto lens for far-off photos, so too many of the Old Testament prophecies are fulfilled immediately, but also in a different, more profound way many years and even centuries later. God immediately fulfilled this prophecy by raising up David's son Solomon who built a magnificent temple in Jerusalem. However, the ultimate fulfilment of this promise is found in Jesus.

Jesus was born in David's royal lineage (see Matthew 1:1-16, Luke 3:23-38), and unlike Solomon, has become the ruler over an eternal Kingdom. Jesus is building the true House of God, not a physical building in Jerusalem, but a people. In the Old Testament God has a temple for His people, but in the New Testament God has a people for His temple.

> "So then you are no longer strangers and aliens, but you are fellow citizens with the saints and members of the household of God, built on the foundation of the apostles and prophets, Christ Jesus himself being the cornerstone, in whom the whole structure, being joined together, grows into a holy temple in the Lord. In him you also are being built together into a dwelling place for God by the Spirit." (Ephesians 2:19-22, ESV)

Jesus calls this people, this House of God, this new temple, the church. He says:

> "I will build My church; and the gates of Hades will not overpower it." (Matthew 16:18, NASB)

Here is the first time the word 'church' is used in the New Testament. It is the name that Jesus chose to describe His people. 'Church' is the Greek word 'ekklesia', which comes from two words: 'ek' meaning 'out', and 'kaleō' meaning 'to call'. So, 'church' literally means an assembly (a gathering) of called out (or summoned) ones. While the word has been used by some to describe a building, the Bible only uses it to describe God's called out people.

Before 'ekklesia' was ever used in a Christian context, it was used to describe a select group of citizens in ancient Athens who had the final say over policies, court rulings, electing state officials and even declaring war. Their authority was extensive. They literally set the course of their civilisation. In a similar way God's "called out ones" - the church - are tasked to bring change, to move in authority and ultimately to "fill the earth and govern it." (Genesis 1:28, NLT)

We also notice that Jesus describes the church as an unstoppable force on earth. When Jesus declared "the gates of Hades will not overpower it", I don't think He was saying that we were being threatened by gates! Who has ever been attacked by a gate? Instead, ask yourself, have I ever found a gate hard to open? Yes, we all have. That's the picture Jesus wants us to understand. The only organisation spiritually equipped to take back territory across this world from the powers of darkness - to burst down its gates, if you will - is the church of Jesus Christ. There is no place where the church can't succeed, because Jesus is building it.

THE PROPHECY OF ISAIAH AND MICAH

In Isaiah 2:2 and Micah 4:1, we read an identical prophecy regarding the House of God.

> "Now it will come about that in the last days the mountain of the house of the LORD will be established as the chief of the mountains, and will be raised above the hills; and all the nations will stream to it." (Isaiah 2:2, NASB)

The fact that Isaiah and Micah both received the same word indicates that "the matter has been firmly decided by God" (Genesis 41:32), see also Deuteronomy 19:15.

Let us unpack the prophecy.

Firstly, the prophecy is for the "last days" which is the era we are currently living in.

Secondly, it relates to the "house of the Lord" which we understand to be the church, the people of God (see 1 Peter 2:5). Jesus taught that the physical House of God (the Temple) in Jerusalem would be replaced by His body, the church (see John 2:19-21). And Paul writes: "Don't you know that you yourselves are God's temple and that God's Spirit dwells in your midst?" (1 Corinthians 3:16, NIV)

The message is clear: in our era, we can expect to see God raise up His people, the church, as chief among the people on earth, and the nations will stream to the church. What an amazing prophecy! The church truly is God's great plan for having an impact on the nations of the world.

> "The church of Jesus Christ is the most important institution in the world. The assembly of the redeemed, the body of Christ, is more significant in world history than any other group or organisation or nation. The United States of America compares to the church of Jesus Christ like a speck of dust compares to the sun. The drama of international relations compares to the mission of the church like a kindergarten riddle compares to Hamlet. All the pomp of May Day in Red Square and all the grandeur new year's celebrations fade into a formless grey in comparison to the splendour of the Bride of Christ." (John Piper)

DANIEL'S DREAM

In the book of Daniel, we again see God speaking of the church, His Plan A.

Daniel was a young God-fearing Jew who, along with many of his people, had been taken captive to Babylon. God promoted Daniel and gave him a position as one of the special advisors to the Babylonian King, Nebuchadnezzar. In Daniel chapter 2 we read that Nebuchadnezzar had a significant dream, which he required his advisors to interpret for him. He made the unreasonable demand that they first tell him the dream before interpreting it. That night, God gave Daniel the same dream. The next day, he was ushered into the King's presence to describe the dream and deliver the interpretation. He told the King that in the dream God showed him "what will take place in the latter days"

(Daniel 2:28), which we know from the New Testament refers to the era in which we live today.

He described how in the dream there was a large state of a man with four distinct parts: the head of gold, the chest and arms of silver, the middle and thighs of bronze and the legs and feet of iron. Daniel went on to say:

> "You continued looking until a stone was cut out without hands, and it struck the statue on its feet of iron and clay and crushed them. Then the iron, the clay, the bronze, the silver and the gold were crushed all at the same time and became like chaff from the summer threshing floors; and the wind carried them away so that not a trace of them was found. **But the stone that struck the statue became a great mountain and filled the whole earth.**" (Daniel 2:34-35, NASB)

Daniel explained to Nebuchadnezzar that each part of the statue represented an empire that would rule the world, the first one being Babylon. History proves that Daniel's prophetic interpretation was accurate:

- The Babylonian Empire
- The Medo-Persian Empire
- The Greek Empire (with Alexander the Great)
- The Roman Empire

He explained that during the fourth world empire, ruled by the Romans: "the God of heaven will set up a kingdom which will never be destroyed…" (Daniel 2:44, NASB).

Daniel prophetically describes the arrival of Jesus and the success of His church, which as we know was birthed during the Roman Empire. Daniel says: **"…the stone that struck the statue became a great mountain and filled the whole earth."** (Daniel 2:35, NASB)

Here is what we glean from Daniel chapter 2:

- World empires will come and go, but God's Kingdom ushered in by the church will grow and be established forever.
- The church prior to the return of Jesus will be like "a great mountain" that will fill "the whole earth." As Paul describes it in Ephesians:

"... the church, which is His body, the fullness of Him who fills all in all." (Ephesians 1:22-23, NASB)

- The church's global success and growth will be because it is the work of God and not the work of man - "a stone was cut out without hands."

More than ever before, we are seeing the church growing to become this "great mountain" that is filling "the whole earth". David B. Barrett and Todd M. Johnson's research into church growth, *"World Christian Trends AD 30-AD 2000"*, revealed that:

Every day on earth there are 100,000 new believers. And every week 4,500 new churches are planted.

The church is God's vision, so the church is our vision. The Go Global family of churches are committed to playing their part in God's great plan. We endeavour to plant and support life-giving churches built on the Word of God and inspired by His Holy Spirit in our nation and across the world. We also want to be a catalyst for unity between churches, with the conviction that such unity in the church paves the way for a spiritual awakening in the world. As Jesus prayed:

"... so that they may be brought to complete unity. Then the world will know that you sent me ..." (John 17:23, NIV)

As we have seen, God has had one mega plan from the very beginning, with the church at its centre. God also has an individual plan for each of our lives. The key to you finding it is to ask how you can play your part in God's mega purpose, the church.

IT'S TIME TO PLAY YOUR PART IN THE CHURCH

When you become a believer in Christ, you automatically become part of the global church family. God is your Father and you now have millions of brothers and sisters. It is an amazing experience to meet a stranger who is a believer anywhere in the world and you instantly feel a God-given connection with them.

The church not only spans the world, it also spans time. It is wonderful to know that the church isn't just made up of believers in our generation, it also includes believers through the ages who are very much alive in heaven (see Hebrews 12:1, 22-23).

Sadly, it is not uncommon to meet believers who say they are part of the 'global church', but are not committed to a local one. Some jump from church to church, never putting their roots down, while others have disconnected from church completely.

> "There can be no Christianity without community." (Nikolaus Ludwig von Zinzendorf)

In the New Testament, there is no example of believers operating independently of a local church. This is one of the reasons why the early church was so effective. As someone once said: "There's nothing as unchristian as a lone Christian." The isolated believer cannot properly fulfil God's plan for their lives if they are operating outside of God's mega plan for the world. Just as a word finds its ultimate use and context as part of a sentence, so too do our lives find meaning in being part of a local church. Just as a part of your body, such as your hand or ear, cannot fulfil its purpose disconnected from your body, so too our gifting and potential is only realised when we are playing our part in the church, which is the Body of Christ (see 1 Corinthians 12:12-31). Not only will a disconnected believer hinder their own purpose, but they will also hinder what God wants to achieve through the church in their generation. Rather, you playing your part will cause the church to advance.

"He makes the whole body fit together perfectly. As each part does its own special work, it helps the other parts grow, so that the whole body is healthy and growing and full of love." (Ephesians 4:15-16, NLT)

If we are to be fully committed to a church, how do we find one? First of all, it helps to know what a local church is supposed to look like. Here's what scripture says:

- A local church ('ekklesia') is a gathering of people. It doesn't matter where this gathering happens, it can be in a large forum (see Acts 5:12), a lecture hall (see Acts 19:9) or a house (see Romans 16:5). The church isn't a building, it's a regular gathering of the people of God.
- A local church has a clear leadership in place which would include pastors and elders (responsible for people), and deacons (responsible for practical duties) and is accountable to apostolic leadership (see Titus 1:5, Acts 14:23, Philippians 1:1, Ephesians 4:11).
- In local church gatherings, you would expect the following to feature regularly: Bible teaching (see 2 Timothy 4:2), breaking bread, worship, prayer, teaching, giving, salvations and baptisms (see Acts 2:42-47).
- A local church plays its part in the Great Commission (see Matthew 28:19-20) by making disciples in their region and beyond (see Philippians 1:3-5, 1 Thessalonians 1:8).
- A local church gathering is a place where the gifts of the Holy Spirit are experienced (see 1 Corinthians 14:26).

Jesus is building His church in our generation. Here are three ways we can commit to playing our part in His great plan:

Commit to church

There are no perfect churches. Yet despite our imperfections, the Bible reveals that Jesus is committed to us, the church. He is so committed, that He calls the church His bride.

So, stop dating the church, it's time to commit!

Let's be like Jesus and commit to an imperfect church.

> "... not abandoning our own meeting together, as is the habit of some people, but encouraging one another; and all the more as you see the day drawing near." (Hebrews 10:25, NASB)

Bad habits ruin us, whilst good habits strengthen our lives. Committing to a church means we're in the good habit of meeting with God's people regularly. Committing to a church means being accountable to the leadership of the church. Committing to a church means that you are there to both receive and contribute.

At the end of these seven studies, we would encourage you to officially commit to becoming an active member of your local church.

Commit to serving in the church

> "As each one has received a special gift, employ it in serving one another as good stewards of the multifaceted grace of God." (1 Peter 4:10, NASB)

God is calling us to use our time and talents to serve others. The church shouldn't be like a cruise ship, where there's a captain and crew but most people are just along for the ride. Effective churches are more like a navy vessel where everyone has a role to play - it's all hands on deck.

To help find the best place to serve in the church, consider two questions:

- Where is there a need? Sometimes we should simply serve to meet a need.
- What are the gifts that God has placed in my life? While we might start serving where there's a need, ultimately, we should seek to serve in a way that lines up with how God has wired us.

Commit to giving to the church

Throughout scripture, we see the principle that God's house should be funded by God's people. Whether it was the Israelites in the wilderness giving towards the Tabernacle (see Exodus 35:29) or providing for the

Levites who ministered on their behalf (see Numbers 18:21). Or whether it was believers resourcing the church, its leaders (see 1 Timothy 5:17), its mission (see Philippians 4:18) or its outreach to the poor (see Acts 4:34-35).

In the Bible, we're called to give in three ways:

- Tithes (the first 10% of your income)
- Offerings (gifts given over above your tithe)
- Alms to the poor (special offerings for individuals or groups in need)

For New Testament believers, tithing isn't to be seen as a law to be obeyed (as we're no longer under the law). Rather, it's a principle of faith to be followed. Just as our father in faith, Abraham tithed as an expression of faith in God, his provider, so too we tithe as a step of faith. Our faith is that Jesus will build His church and that God will provide our needs.

> "The New Testament Christian is liberated from the law of tithing into the Spirit of sacrificial and generous giving." (Sam Storms)

The tithe wasn't just about the amount, it was about your priorities. It wasn't just 10% of your income, it was to be the first 10% of your income, or the "first fruit". Some people consider tithing at the end of the month with what is left over. However, biblically the tithe should be the first 10% (see Exodus 23:19, Proverbs 3:9-10, 1 Corinthians 16:2). It takes faith to give the first 10%, trusting that God will bless the 90% that's left - and He does. The Bible is full of promises of how God will provide abundantly for those who prioritise giving to the church:

> "Bring the whole tithe into the storehouse, that there may be food in my house. Test me in this," says the Lord Almighty, "and see if I will not throw open the floodgates of heaven and pour out so much blessing that there will not be room enough to store it." (Malachi 3:10, NIV)

And again in 2 Corinthians, scripture promises that God will give to givers and will resource those who resource His House:

> "And God is able to make all grace abound to you, so that having all sufficiency in all things at all times, you may abound in every good work. As it is written, "He has distributed freely, he has given to the poor; his righteousness endures forever." He who supplies seed to the sower and bread for food will supply and multiply your seed for sowing and increase the harvest of your righteousness. You will be enriched in every way to be generous in every way, which through us will produce thanksgiving to God." (2 Corinthians 9:8-11, ESV)

In Go Global, we ask believers to tithe to their local churches, and in turn the churches tithe their income back to Go Global. This giving enables Go Global to fund the establishment of new churches and the support of existing churches all across the world. We truly believe that Jesus is building His church and we get to play our part in filling the earth and ushering in His Kingdom.

We hope this study has inspired your faith. God truly has a huge plan for His church. Let's all play our part with passion in seeing His dream become a reality.

FREQUENTLY ASKED QUESTIONS

WHAT STYLE AND FORM OF CHURCH IS BEST AND MOST BIBLICAL?

When deciding what makes a good church, there are primary and secondary considerations. The primary consideration is what does the Bible say about church life. The secondary considerations have to do with our preferences or practical circumstances.

The Bible is clear on many aspects of church life, such as the importance of:

- A local leadership team (comprised of elders, deacons and others)
- Ministry gifts operating in a church (see Ephesians 4:11)
- The gifts of the Holy Spirit in gatherings
- Bible teaching, prayer and worship
- Regularly breaking bread
- Making disciples
- Believers' baptism
- Genuine love and generosity between believers

These matters are of primary importance and are non-negotiable for a healthy church.

However, many issues relating to a church's style or form are secondary considerations. Here are some examples:

- Whether a church gathers in a large venue or homes
- Whether the worship style is traditional or contemporary
- Whether the church adopts a formal or relaxed dress code
- Whether a church is multisite or meets in one place
- The day and time a church chooses to meet

The Bible is deliberately non-prescriptive on such secondary matters.

There is a problem when people place higher importance on secondary matters, yet neglect primary matters. **Form is always secondary; biblical culture is always primary.**

In Go Global we are a family of churches committed to a shared theology, and yet our churches vary widely in style and form.

ARE DENOMINATIONS A GOOD THING?

In the early church, there were no denominations, however over time, divisions - sometimes known as schisms - emerged within the church which gave rise to the large number of Christian denominations we have today. Are these multiple expressions of church a good thing?

The Bible is clear that we should endeavour to have unity among God's people (see Psalm 133 and Ephesians 4:3). However, the unity that scripture encourages, is always on the basis, and never at the expense, of truth. In fact, Paul taught that sometimes for the sake of truth there needs to be division:

> "For there also have to be factions among you, so that those who are approved may become evident among you." (1 Corinthians 11:19, NASB)

At various points in church history, it has been necessary for there to be division for the sake of truth.

On 31 October 1517, it was necessary for a German monk called Martin Luther to nail a document to the door of a church building in Wittenberg. The document, now known as Luther's '95 Theses', put into writing his strong disagreements with some of the unbiblical practices and beliefs of the mainstream Catholic Church of his time. Luther's protest against unbiblical Christianity gave rise not only to the Lutheran Church but also to all Protestant denominations around the world. This division was necessary to preserve the purity of biblical Christianity.

Throughout church history, there have been many battles over truth that have given rise to different groupings and denominations. While we do not rejoice in division, we realise that sometimes division is necessary for truth to be restored to the church at large. Here are some examples of truths being restored as denominations and groupings were created:

- The Presbyterians formed and reminded us that churches are to be led by a team and not by a solitary leader
- The Baptists formed and reminded us that believers are to be baptised by full immersion
- The Pentecostals formed and reminded us of the importance of being baptised with the Holy Spirit

Practically speaking, different churches also reach different people. The rich variety of styles and forms of church provides us with an opportunity to reach different parts of society.

While much good has come from the various groupings and denominations, there is also a negative side.

Jesus's prayer for believers was "that they may all be one ... so that the world may believe that You sent Me." (John 17:21, NASB). Disunity and denominationalism undermine the church's witness to the world. The question is: can we be united with others who are theologically different? The answer is yes. If the differences are around non-salvation issues (worship style, the form of baptism practised, different views on leadership and church governance, etc.), then there can be unity. However, if the differences are around salvation issues (the definition of sin, the nature of God, the gospel, the authority of scripture, etc.), then sadly there is no truth foundation on which true Christian unity can be built.

As a family of churches, Go Global is non-denominational. We desire to get back to a New Testament model, where churches worked in relationship because of shared apostolic ministry and teaching, not because of their denomination. We are a family of autonomous churches united in relationship, based on our shared vision, values and theology, as outlined in this book. In Go Global, one of our core values is to love 'the church', not just our church. So, wherever we exist as churches, we actively seek to be catalysts for unity among biblical churches. We desire to see the church across the world in its various forms unite and succeed for the glory of God.

WITH SO MANY STORIES OF HYPOCRISY AND SCANDAL, CAN THE CHURCH STILL BE TRUSTED?

One of the most shocking books in the Old Testament is Hosea. In it, God instructs Hosea to marry a prostitute named Gomer and to remain faithful to her even though she is consistently unfaithful to him. God was making a prophetic point to the people of Israel that He was faithful to them even when they were not faithful to Him.

In the New Testament, Jesus addresses seven churches in The Book of Revelation. Some were compromising with sin, off track in their theology, or had lost sight of their passion for God. Yet even in His rebuke, He affirms that "Those whom I love I rebuke and discipline" (Revelation 3:19).

It is clear that God, who is perfect, is patient and gracious with His people who are often far from perfect. He rebukes and challenges them to change, but He never rejects them.

In light of this, it would not be appropriate for us, with our own imperfections, to reject the church for its many failings. So, let's not reject what God will never reject. Let's not pull down what Jesus said He would build (see Matthew 16:18). Let's love what God loves - His church.

Having said this, it is clear that Jesus calls His church to higher standards of integrity, especially at a leadership level. Paul in 1st Timothy chapter 3, speaks to leaders at great length regarding their behaviour and example. He talks to them about having integrity in their marriages, their money, their alcohol consumption and their private life. He also makes it clear that leaders who step out of line should experience church discipline (see 1 Timothy 5:19-20). When a leader has seriously stumbled in their behaviour, Paul is clear it should be handled in the open rather than behind closed doors.

In some circumstances, the leader being disciplined will need to step back from their role for a period. In more serious cases, they should be permanently removed from ministry. But in all cases, when there is repentance, thank God, there is hope, forgiveness and grace, with the acceptance of God and the church.

No church leader at any level should be unaccountable. In a local church, the leadership should be accountable to the church and to each other, but also to external apostolic oversight. Apostolic leaders should function within a team and never in isolation to ensure they are also accountable. For example, Paul challenged the apostle Peter's hypocritical behaviour (see Galatians 2:11-13).

IF THE CHURCH IS GOD'S 'PLAN A', HOW DOES ISRAEL FIT INTO IT?

There are two extreme views often presented by Christians when it comes to the question of Israel. There are some Christians who believe that the church has replaced Israel in God's purpose and that now they are just another nation in the nations of the world. This position is called 'Replacement Theology.' And there are others on the other extreme, called 'Christian Zionists', who strongly emphasise the active role of the Jewish people in God's purposes on earth. Some Zionists would hold to the belief that Jewish people can be saved through obeying the Law of Moses, and others even believe that the temple will again be rebuilt in Jerusalem.

Here are some reflections from scripture which present a middle ground between the two extremes described above.

God has only ever had one people. In Genesis, God promised Abraham that his offspring would become a great and numerous people who would bring blessing to the whole earth. In the New Testament, we learn that this promise referred not primarily to his physical descendants, but his spiritual descendants - those who live with the same faith as Abraham (see Romans 4:16 and Galatians 3:29).

The apostle Peter uses language from Exodus chapter 19 that describes the Jewish people to describe the church, which is made up of people from all nationalities:

> "But you are a chosen race, a royal priesthood, a holy nation, a people for God's own possession, so that you may proclaim the excellencies of Him who has called you out of darkness into His marvellous light; for you once were not a people, but now you are the people of God ..." (1 Peter 2:9-10, NASB)

Likewise, the apostle Paul calls all believers in Jesus the 'Israel of God,' no matter their ethnicity:

> "Neither circumcision nor uncircumcision means anything; what counts is the new creation. Peace and mercy to all who follow this rule - to the Israel of God." (Galatians 6:15-16, NIV)

So, has the church replaced Israel? If we mean, has the church now taken the place of the Jewish people, thus demoting them to being merely just another nation among the nations? The answer is no. But if we mean - has the church replaced 'spiritual Israel'? The answer would be - the church *is* 'spiritual Israel'.

'Spiritual Israel,' the true people of God, have always and only been the people of faith. In the Old Testament, many of the Jewish people were the people of God, but not all (see Romans 9:6). In fact, there are many examples of non-Jewish people of God in the Old Testament, here are some:

- Rahab, the Canaanite prostitute (see Joshua 2).

- Ruth, the Moabite (see the book of Ruth).
- Obed-Edom, who stored the Ark of the Covenant at his property, was a Gittite from Gath (see 2 Samuel 6).
- Naaman, the Aramean commander who came to Elisha for healing (see 2 Kings 5).

It is important to also address some of the wrong beliefs that some Christian Zionists promote.

Some believe that there are two ways to be saved - a Jew can be saved through obeying the Law of Moses and everyone be saved by trusting in Jesus. However, the Bible is clear there is only one way to be saved - through Jesus (see Romans 3:20 and Galatians 2:16). The blood Jesus shed on the cross is sufficient to cover the sin of all people who ever lived or ever will live, whether they lived BC or AD.

> "Many people falsely assume that only New Testament believers are saved by grace whereas Old Testament believers were saved by their obedience to the law of Moses and not by grace. The truth is that both the Old and New Testaments teach that everyone who is saved, throughout all history, is saved the same way: by grace, through faith, on account of Christ alone." (Hank Hanegraaff)

Another belief that some hold is that there are two active covenants. This again is biblically inaccurate. The Old Covenant, the relationship God established with Israel in the Old Testament, was in place to prepare the world for Jesus. But when Jesus shed His blood, a New Covenant was in place, which made "obsolete" the previous covenant.

> "By calling this covenant "new," he has made the first one obsolete ..." (Hebrews 8:13, NIV)

In summary, there is only one Saviour, one covenant and one people of God.

But the question remains, does God still have a plan for the Jewish people, or are they just the same as all the other nations in God's sight?

In Romans chapters 9 to 11, Paul explains at great lengths God's plans for the Jewish people. In these chapters, he uses the word 'Israel' sometimes in reference to ethnic Jews and other times in reference to those who are the international people of God by faith. What is clear from these chapters is that God has not finished with the Jewish nation. Indeed, Paul gives us the hope that there will be a revival among ethnic Jews, before Jesus' return.

> "For I do not want you, brothers and sisters, to be uninformed of this mystery — so that you will not be wise in your own estimation — that a partial hardening has happened to Israel until the fullness of the Gentiles has come in; and so all Israel will be saved ..." (Romans 11:25-26, NASB)

Just as Joseph was sold by his brothers into slavery yet went on to be the ruler who would rescue much of the ancient world from famine, so too Jesus, who was rejected by His own people, has become the Saviour of the world. In the account of Joseph, it wasn't his brothers who first came for help in famine, it was the rest of the world. But eventually, in their desperation, his brothers came to be saved and bow the knee. I believe this story acts as a picture of what God has been doing in history. The Jewish 'rejection' of Jesus has "brought reconciliation to the world" (Romans 11:15). As the gospel is having an impact on the nations of the world, a point will come and may have already started to happen, when the Jewish people will, at last, acknowledge their Messiah. Since the turn of the millennium, there has been a notable increase in the number of Jewish people putting their faith in Jesus and Messianic congregations being established. Research published in 2022 showed that the Israeli Messianic movement has more than tripled in the last 20 years (source: Alec Goldberg and David Serner, in Jesus-Believing Israelis: Exploring Messianic Fellowships). Indeed we believe, "the last will be first, and the first will be last" (Matthew 20:16).

Before being crucified Jesus declared to the Jewish nation:

> "Jerusalem, Jerusalem, you who kill the prophets and stone those sent to you, how often I have longed to gather your children together, as a hen gathers her chicks under her wings, and you were not willing. Look, your

house is left to you desolate. For I tell you, you will not see me again until you say, 'Blessed is he who comes in the name of the Lord.'" (Matthew 23:37-39, NIV)

Jesus speaks of a day when many Jewish people will at last acknowledge Jesus by saying "Blessed is he who comes in the name of the Lord". Such a final recognition of their Messiah will be a clear sign that they will 'see' Him 'again' in His great and final return.

Jesus also predicted that in His generation, Jerusalem and the temple would be destroyed (see Matthew 24). He was right - this happened in AD 70. This event was clearly God's judgement on the Jewish nation for their rejection of the Messiah (see Luke 19:41-44). From our vantage point in history, in the past century, we have witnessed, against all odds, Israel being reinstated to their land in 1948. It is fair to assume that if God removed them from their land in AD 70, it is also by God's permission and plan that they were reinstated in 1948.

There seems to be an emerging pattern, a historical mirror image:

- **Jesus comes** (2000 years ago)
- **Jews reject** (they crucify their Messiah)
- Removed from **the land** (AD 70)
- Back in **the land** (1948)
- **Jews accept** (many at last turn to Jesus)
- **Jesus comes** (in His return)

It would be wrong to deem the Jewish nation to be just another nation. To do so would be to ignore their heritage, their history and most importantly their immense contribution to the world. Paul wrote:

"Theirs is the adoption to sonship; theirs the divine glory, the covenants, the receiving of the law, the temple worship and the promises. Theirs are the patriarchs, and from them is traced the human ancestry of the Messiah, who is God overall, forever praised! Amen." (Romans 9:4-5)

In summary:

- God has always had just one people.
- In the last 2000 years, that people have been called 'the church' (see Matthew 16:18).
- The church is made up of believers in Jesus from all backgrounds (Jew or Gentile).
- The scripture points to a future hope that the Jewish people who have such a rich heritage and history will once again finally acknowledge that Jesus is indeed the Messiah - this should be our earnest hope and prayer.

THE JESUS LEADERSHIP MODEL

Jesus is the greatest leader who ever walked this earth. And yet, His leadership ethos was fundamentally different to the world's version of leadership. Jesus instructed His disciples:

> "You know that the rulers of the Gentiles lord it over them, and their high officials exercise authority over them. Not so with you. Instead, whoever wants to become great among you must be your servant, and whoever wants to be first must be your slave - just as the Son of Man did not come to be served, but to serve, and to give his life as a ransom for many." (Matthew 20:25-28, NIV)

So instead of overpowering people, Jesus says that leaders are to empower people. Instead of domineering people, leaders are to serve those under their care. Jesus not only taught this, He modelled it in the most remarkable way:

> "Do nothing out of selfish ambition or vain conceit. Rather, in humility value others above yourselves, not looking to your own interests but each of you to the interests of the others. In your relationships with one another, have the same mindset as Christ Jesus: Who, being in very nature God, did not consider equality with God something to be used to

his own advantage; rather, he made himself nothing by taking the very nature of a servant, being made in human likeness. And being found in appearance as a man, he humbled himself by becoming obedient to death - even death on a cross! Therefore God exalted him to the highest place and gave him the name that is above every name, that at the name of Jesus every knee should bow, in heaven and on earth and under the earth, and every tongue acknowledge that Jesus Christ is Lord, to the glory of God the Father." (Philippians 2:3-11, NIV)

He who is the highest of the high became the lowest of the low. He served us, by doing what was necessary for us, by dying on our behalf. His leadership of people was expressed in His serving of people. His leadership was driven by love. In practice, He valued others above Himself, doing for them what they couldn't do for themselves. What a leader!

"True greatness, true leadership, is found in giving yourself in service to others, not in coaxing or inducing others to serve you." (J. Oswald Sanders)

Leaders should make it their ambition to be able to say with the apostle Paul: "Imitate me, just as I imitate Christ" (1 Corinthians 11:1).

In the light of Jesus' teaching and example, there is no place in church leadership for egotistical, arrogant, harsh and controlling behaviour. Instead, leaders in the church should aspire to be:

- Strong, but not harsh (see 2 Timothy 4:2)
- Directive, but not controlling or dominating
- Driven by love and not by ego (see 2 Corinthians 5:14)
- Confident, but not arrogant
- Visible, but always pointing to Jesus

"The authority by which the Christian leader leads is not power but love, not force but example, not coercion but reasoned persuasion. Leaders have power, but power is safe only in the hands of those who humble themselves to serve." (John Stott)

As we consider the leadership titles in the New Testament, it is important to say that title follows function, not the other way round. Too many people desire a title only to find themselves in leadership roles that they aren't called to. It is far better to start serving God's people and work in your calling first - the title will then follow. For example, a potential elder should have a track record of humbly functioning in an eldership capacity among God's people before being officially given the title.

We desire to build our lives and churches on God's word. When it comes to a church leadership structure, we're committed to following the pattern and design found in the New Testament. Our conviction is that if we want to see God's results, we should build according to God's plan.

Here's what we see in scripture:

EPHESIANS 4 MINISTRIES

> ""When He ascended on high, He led captive the captives, and He gave gifts to people …" He who descended is Himself also He who ascended far above all the heavens, so that He might fill all things. And He gave some as apostles, some as prophets, some as evangelists, some as pastors and teachers, for the equipping of the saints for the work of ministry, for the building up of the body of Christ; until we all attain to the unity of the faith, and of the knowledge of the Son of God, to a mature man, to the measure of the stature which belongs to the fullness of Christ." (Ephesians 4:8, 10-13, NASB)

Why did Jesus descend? Why did He come from heaven to earth, from the throne to the manger, from the joys of heaven to the pain and disgrace of the cross? And why did He ascend? Why did He rise from death, ascend to heaven and ultimately ascend to the eternal throne?

The answer is, as Paul writes in his letter to the Ephesians, "so that He might fill all things," which has been God's purpose from the beginning (see Study 4). Theologian and writer, William Barclay, said: "He did not ascend on high to leave the world but to fill the world with His presence."

God's great purpose through the life, death, resurrection and ascension of Jesus is to "fill all things." God intends that the church is to be "… His body, the fullness of Him who fills all in all." (Ephesians 1:23, NASB) And now we discover that to accomplish this purpose He has given "some as apostles, some as prophets, some as evangelists, some as pastors and teachers."

> "… Christ has given these ministers as part of the overall purpose for which He ascended - that His work of filling all things might be brought to completion … Christ's giving of ministers of the word to build up the whole Body into His fulness is interwoven with the goal of His pervading the cosmos with His presence and rule." (Andrew T Lincoln, New Testament scholar)

When Jesus was on earth, He was the complete leader:

- He's the apostle (see Hebrews 3:1)
- He's the prophet (see John 6:14)
- He's the evangelist (see Luke 19:10)
- He's the pastor (see John 10:11)
- He's the teacher (see John 13:13)

Whatever your need, be it teaching, prophetic direction, or apostolic strategy Jesus was your one-stop shop. He embodied all of these essential giftings.

When Jesus ascended, scripture says that "He gave gifts to people." This means that even though Jesus is now physically in heaven, His five-fold ministry continues on earth through leaders whom He has called. Indeed, they will continue "until we all attain to the unity of the faith, and of the knowledge of the Son of God, to a mature man, to the measure of the stature which belongs to the fullness of Christ."

These leaders aren't just gifted people, they are gifts. After all, the Bible says, "He gave some as …". With this in mind, we must show due appreciation for the gifts He's given, praying for and honouring the leaders in our midst.

We also see that these gifts of leaders come from Jesus and always point to Jesus. At school, you may have seen the physics demonstration where light is passed into a prism. The pure white light enters the prism and exits out the other side as the spectrum of colours. Likewise, the perfect ministry of Jesus has now been separated out and distributed to leaders. The experiment continues with a second prism being placed so that the colours enter the prism and then exit as pure white light. In the same way, the five-fold ministry gifts are to produce Christ-likeness in the people of God (Ephesians 4:13).

God's desire is for churches to be balanced, not lopsided. If a church is led by a pastor, the people may be well cared for but could soon become inward-looking if there's no apostolic visionary input. If an evangelist leads a church, many people will come, but without the necessary support of pastoral leaders, the church might lose people just as fast as it gain them. If a prophet leads a church, the people will surely be inspired and very sensitive to the leading of the Holy Spirit, however without the gift of a Bible teacher, they could go off track theologically. Like a hand has five fingers, God wants every local church to be connected with all five ministry gifts. This doesn't mean that every church has all five residing in the church (certainly in the early stages), but it does mean that every local congregation should welcome ministries that complement the strengths and gifts that are there. This cross-fertilisation of ministries is seen in the early church as described in the New Testament. God doesn't want independent churches, but rather interdependent churches that are part of apostolic families of churches. Together we all win.

Let us now look in more detail at each of these gifts.

Apostles

Jesus specifically called twelve of His disciples 'apostles', which means those "sent out" with a mission. The original twelve apostles were unique and in Revelation are referred to as the "apostles of the Lamb" (Revelation 21:14).

In the book of Acts, we discover that many others were also given the title 'apostle'. The most famous was Paul, who, when he was called Saul, had been a persecutor of the church before his conversion. Other apostles mentioned are:

- Barnabas (see Acts 14:4)
- James, the half-brother of Jesus and leader of the Jerusalem church (see Galatians 1:19)
- Silas (see 1 Thessalonians 2:6 links to Acts 17:1-4)
- Apollos (see 1 Corinthians 4:6-9)
- Epaphroditus (see Philippians 2:25, the word "messenger" in Greek is the word "apostle")
- Two unnamed apostles (see 2 Corinthians 8:23, where again "messenger" translates to "apostle")
- Andronicus and Junias (see Romans 16:7)

Apostles, working with prophets, are foundational leaders who play an essential role in planting and establishing churches. Paul writes that the church is:

"... built on the foundation of the apostles and prophets, with Christ Jesus himself as the chief cornerstone." (Ephesians 2:20, NIV)

In the New Testament, we see many examples of apostles laying foundations in churches:

- The foundation of Jesus Christ and His gospel (see Matthew 16:16-18, Romans 15:20, 1 Corinthians 3:10-11).
- The foundation of biblical truth (see Acts 2:42).
- The foundation of being filled with the Holy Spirit (see Acts 8:14-15).
- The foundation of a local leadership team (see Titus 1:5).

A common question is: "Is your church part of a denomination, or is it an independent church?" The answer is "neither!" Equally, we could ask whether the church in Ephesus (or Corinth, or Philippi) is part of a denomination, or was it an independent church? The answer, again, would be neither. In the New Testament, we don't see church denominations, nor do we see independent churches. We see churches working together in relationship with apostolic leaders. And that's what we desire to be in our generation.

> "In denominationalism, people gather when they agree, and they divide when they disagree. But with apostolic movements people rally around fathers and family." (Kris Vallotton)

Once a church has been planted, the apostle's next priority is to establish a local leadership team. Paul and Barnabas travelled through the churches that they'd just planted, and "... appointed elders for them in each church ... with prayer and fasting ..." (Acts 14:23, NIV)

Just as a father traditionally gives away his daughter in marriage, entrusting the primary leadership and care of his daughter to the husband, so too the primary leadership authority for the church passes to local elders from the apostles upon appointment.

Does this mean that the apostles no longer have authority in the church? Not at all. The apostles continue to work with local churches relationally, providing support, advice and even challenge. Just as a foundation is essential at the start of a construction project, so it continues to be vital throughout the lifespan of the building. Apostles continue to provide relational support and oversight to churches once they are up and running. We see this in Paul's letters, which were fatherly encouragements providing ongoing support to local churches and leaders. The apostle's authority and wisdom are now invited and welcomed in the church by the local leaders. Indeed, it would be a foolish leadership team that rejected being under apostolic oversight and chose to operate independently and unaccountably.

Typically, apostles will also have another Ephesians 4 gift operating in their lives alongside their apostolic calling. For example, Paul was an apostle and a teacher, while Barnabas was an apostle and a prophet (see Acts 13:1). Peter was an apostle and a pastor or shepherd (see John 21:15-17).

Furthermore, we see that there was a variety of ways that apostles chose to operate. While some apostles such as Paul operated as itinerant leaders - travelling from place to place - others based themselves in local churches, and from these apostolic hubs impacted the regions beyond (for example, James who was based in Jerusalem, see Acts 15, yet his impact was felt by Jewish converts and churches in the regions beyond, see James 1:1).

Throughout much of church history, the foundational ministry of apostles and prophets has been forgotten and even denied. People would commonly speak of pastors, teachers and evangelists, but apostles and prophets often weren't mentioned. This is ironic considering that in the New Testament, 'apostle' is mentioned 132 times, and 'prophet' 140 times, whereas 'evangelist' is only mentioned three times and 'pastor' only once! Nevertheless, God has been raising up apostles through the generations to birth church movements and to advance His Kingdom on earth. Great leaders and reformers, such as Martin Luther, Nikolaus Zinzendorf and John Wesley were certainly apostolic, yet would never have been called this or have used this title themselves. In recent times, the biblical conviction that there are modern-day apostles has become far more widespread, leading to noticeable fruit and growth in the Body of Christ. As Peter Wagner, a key leader in the Church Growth Movement observed:

> "The new apostolic reformation is an extraordinary work of God at the close of the 20th Century, which is, to a significant extent, changing the shape of Protestant Christianity around the world. In virtually every region of the world, these new apostolic churches constitute the fastest growing segment of Christianity... this is the day of the most radical change in the way of doing church since the Protestant Reformation."

Prophets

'Prophet' in Greek is the word 'prophetas' which comes from two words: 'pro', meaning 'ahead', and 'phemi', meaning 'to declare'. So, a prophet is someone who speaks God's word to prepare you for what's coming.

The role of a prophet is crucial in seeing churches and individuals move forward. We recognise that prophets alongside apostles help found and establish churches (see Ephesians 2:20).

The Old Testament gives us many more examples of how prophets function. We see them bringing challenge and comfort to God's people. We also see them cheering on leaders charged with God-given work. For example, Zechariah prophesied and brought encouragement to Zerubbabel when he was struggling with the task of rebuilding the temple in Jerusalem (see Zechariah 4:6-10). We also see the prophet Nathan encouraging King David concerning his future legacy (see 2 Samuel 7:12-14).

In the New Testament, we see prophets working closely with apostles and churches. In Acts, Agabus delivered a prophecy concerning a famine that was coming in Judea. This resulted in Paul and Barnabus raising funds and delivering a large donation to those who would be affected. We also see apostles travelling with prophets to encourage and build up churches (see Acts 15:30-35).

Prophetic encouragement, direction and challenge, will protect leaders from quitting under pressure, will help churches avoid unseen dangers, and will confirm God's will in decisions that are being made.

For prophets and prophecies to be safe two things need to be in place. Firstly, prophets need to function with accountability as part of a team and alongside church leaders and apostles. Secondly, all prophecies need to be weighed by other church leaders and ultimately by scripture.

Evangelists

The word 'evangelist' means 'a bringer of good news'. An evangelist is someone whom God has empowered and equipped to effectively share the good news of the gospel and see many coming to Christ.

As well as sharing the gospel with people outside the church, the evangelist is also called to train and equip believers to be evangelistic and share the gospel.

"He gave some as apostles, some as prophets, some as evangelists, some as pastors and teachers, for the equipping of the saints for the work of ministry ..." (Ephesians 4:11-12, NASB)

What is the biggest fruit of an evangelist? Is it the multitudes of people who have become believers? While this is wonderful, the greatest fruit is the army of believers who are now actively sharing the good news with their communities.

As the old Chinese proverb goes: "Give a man a fish you feed him for a day. Teach a man to fish and you feed him for a lifetime". An evangelist doesn't just bring the new converts in, they train believers to do the same.

Pastors

While we have got used to the title 'pastor', a proper - and more helpful - translation of the Greek word 'poimen' is actually 'shepherd'.

Jesus is the ultimate Pastor/Shepherd of the sheep. He calls Himself the "Good Shepherd" who "lays down His life for the sheep" (John 10:11). In the same way pastors in the church are to sacrificially serve and lead God's people.

Jesus is also called the Chief Shepherd. Peter encourages pastors and elders:

"Be shepherds of God's flock that is under your care, watching over them - not because you must, but because you are willing, as God wants you to be; not pursuing dishonest gain, but eager to serve; not lording it over those entrusted to you, but being examples to the flock. And when the Chief Shepherd appears, you will receive the crown of glory that will never fade away." (1 Peter 5:2-4, NIV)

Psalm 23 famously describes how God leads us as a Shepherd. In the same way, pastors are to help people:

- Experience soul restoration
- Make right choices

- Avoid sin and spiritual danger
- Get through the dark valleys of life
- Step into a blessed future

Even though people will deeply appreciate their support, a pastor must always be careful to point people to Jesus, to help people become Jesus-dependent, not pastor-dependent.

As a church develops and grows, a team of pastors (some of whom are elders) should be in place to care for God's people.

Teachers

It is the truth that sets people free, so the gift of a teacher in the church is vital in making sure the church is spiritually healthy, growing and free.

The Bible gives a strong caution to teachers stating that those "... who teach will be judged more strictly." (James 3:1). Teachers are to be Bible teachers, not teachers of opinion. They're not to teach their thoughts but God's thoughts (see 2 Timothy 4:2 and 1 Peter 4:11).

The gift of a teacher in scripture can be seen as a gift that functions locally (in a church) and trans-locally (across churches). In a local church setting, while different leaders can be involved with teaching, the elders in particular are to be "able to teach" (1 Timothy 3:2). Paul and Apollos were examples of teachers whose impact was trans-local. They travelled from church to church while Paul also made an impact through his writing. Today, it is so important for great teachers to emerge locally within churches, but we're also grateful to God for the many anointed teachers that He's raised up to be a blessing across churches.

ELDERS AND PASTORS

While a small church is led by a leader, a growing church is led by a leader and a team. In the New Testament, we see that churches were led by teams. Typically, there would be a more prominent leader who would lead the team. For example, James led the team and the church in Jerusalem, while Timothy led the team and the church in Ephesus.

The leadership team in the church is made up of a collection of different leaders, including elders, pastors and deacons (see Philippians 1:1).

As we've previously seen, for the apostles it was a high priority to have a team of elders in place in each church. Paul considered a church "unfinished" until an eldership was appointed (see Titus 1:5).

In the New Testament, there are three words used to describe elders:

"Episkopos," which translates overseer

The word is in two parts - 'epi' meaning 'over', and 'skopéō' meaning 'scope'. Putting these words together we get 'scope over' or 'overseer'.

An elder cannot just be interested in their area of church; they need to show a concern to 'scope over' the whole church.

The word 'overseer' speaks of the calling of an elder to rule, to have authority and to set the direction.

"Presbuteros," which translates elder

The word 'elder' has strong links with Jewish culture. In synagogues and Jewish communities, they would have been elders. The title infers seniority and maturity within the group. We understand that maturity in God is not necessarily linked to age but to the depth of their faith.

The elders, as those who are spiritually mature, are to help others grow through teaching truth and also be able to refute error.

"Poimen," which translates shepherd (or pastor)

All elders are to be pastors and are to provide pastoral care and protection for God's people.

While all elders are pastors, not all pastors are necessarily appointed as elders. Within a church, pastors and elders are to function together as a team to provide care for God's people.

DEACONS

Within the church leadership team are the deacons. While elders and pastors directly look after people, deacons look after areas of responsibility.

In Greek, the word for 'deacon' is 'diakonos' which translates as 'servant'. Deacons carry senior responsibility for practical serving in the church.

In the New Testament, we're given the example in Acts 6:1-7 of deacons who were put in place to provide food to poor widows in the Jerusalem church.

While the Bible spells out the character qualities of a potential deacon (see 1 Timothy 3:8-13), there is deliberately less detail on how they should function in a church. This gives room and permission for churches to decide how deacons can best serve in their context. For some, the deacons will oversee the food distribution to the poor, for others, deacons will carry some of the practical running of church gatherings. Others will release deacons to help with administration. The options are limitless, but the calling is the same - they are senior servants carrying responsibilities in the House of God.

VOLUNTEER LEADERSHIP ROLES

Gone are the days when a church is led and run by a professional, theologically trained leader, who does everything for everyone. This outdated model kept churches small and limited the potential of the members. We believe that the church is a body, and everyone has a part to play. Indeed, the church grows as everyone plays their part (see Ephesians 4:16).

We want to foster a releasing culture, where church members are given an opportunity to contribute and grow their gifts in serving and ministry. This ethos enables churches to grow and leaders to emerge.

While the Bible provides us with clear leadership titles and categories (as outlined earlier in this study), in a growing church there will be many other volunteer leadership roles which will by necessity emerge to help the church function.

Some examples would include:

- Small group or home group leaders
- Hospitality team leader
- Welcome, ushering and stewarding team leader
- Evangelism team leader
- Intercession team leader
- Youth leader

It has been our experience that people who eventually become elders, pastors or teachers first learned to serve faithfully with a smaller pastoral responsibility, for example by leading a discipleship small group or a house church. In turn, people who become great deacons first learned to serve in practical areas of church life. The principle is:

"The one who is faithful in a very little thing is also faithful in much ..." (Luke 16:10, NASB)

This list of volunteer leadership roles is unlimited, and titles will vary from place to place. But the heart behind these roles is the same: we want to mobilise an army of leaders to see individuals and the whole church grow.

OUR RESPONSE

Be like Jesus; be a servant

Whether we have a title or not, whether we are seen by others or not, let's have a desire to be like Jesus and to serve others.

Jesus said: "... whoever wants to become great among you must be your servant, and whoever wants to be first must be your slave ..." (Matthew 20:26-27, NIV)

Notice that Jesus doesn't rebuke us for the desire to be great, instead, He teaches us how to become great, God's way. The desire to be great, the desire to make a difference, and the desire to play our part in a bigger story, is a God-given desire.

Commit today to being a servant of God who serves people and serves the church.

> "An individual has not started living until he can rise above the narrow confines of his individualistic concerns to the broader concerns of all humanity. Life's most persistent and urgent question is 'What are you doing for others?' Everybody can be great. Because anybody can serve." (Martin Luther King)

Value the leaders God has placed in your life

In the world, it's common for people to criticise and slander leaders in politics, in education or in the workplace. But in God's kingdom, there's a different culture we are to aspire to. Scripture says:

> "Obey your leaders and submit to them - for they keep watch over your souls as those who will give an account - so that they may do this with joy, not groaning; for this would be unhelpful for you." (Hebrews 13:17, NASB)

Leaders must serve, value and honour those they are leading, this is true leadership. We discover that leaders will have to "give an account" to God for how they treat people.

It's also vital for us to honour those who lead us in the Lord.

Honouring means we speak well of leaders, pray for them, and carry their advice with weight. Honouring means if we have a problem with them, we don't slip into sinful gossip but instead, we have the courage to raise the issue with them directly.

Honouring Jesus, the ultimate leader, is easy - He's perfect! However, honouring church leaders, who are imperfect, isn't as easy. Sometimes it requires us to have grace for them, just as we'd want others to have grace for us.

Honouring leadership brings the best out in leaders. When Jesus visited His hometown of Nazareth, they dishonoured Him and His calling (see Mark 6:4). The result was that "He could not do any miracles there" (Mark 6:5). When we dishonour leaders, we deny ourselves of the benefit and the blessing that God has for us through their leadership.

So, let's commit to a different culture, a culture of honour, love and mutual respect. In such a culture, both the church and its leaders go further.

Consider becoming a leader

In a growing church, there is lots of space for people to move into leadership. Indeed, typically churches are crying out for leaders.

How do you become a leader?

- Firstly, be a good follower. Follow Jesus closely and honour the church leaders over you.
- Secondly, seek to serve. If you're not willing to serve, then you're not ready to lead.
- Thirdly, allow God to work on your character. Who you are in secret is more important than who you are in public. You don't have to be perfect to be a leader (no one is), but to be a leader means to walk with integrity and to repent of your sins.
- Fourthly, share your desire to lead with your church leaders. Allow the church leaders to train you and to help you find your place as a leader.

FREQUENTLY ASKED QUESTIONS

WHEN SHOULD I ASK FOR A LEADER'S ADVICE?

When it comes to the bigger choices we make in life, it is always wise to involve others. As the Book of Proverbs says:

> "Listen to counsel, receive instruction, and accept correction, that you may be wise in the time to come." (Proverbs 19:20, AMP)

> "The way of fools seems right to them, but the wise listen to advice." (Proverbs 12:15, NIV)

While it is good to listen to the advice of others, it is important to note that not everyone's opinion is equal. There are certain people that God has placed in our lives who spiritually have authority and therefore their words of counsel should carry more weight than others. For example:

- A husband as the spiritual head of the marriage
- Parents are to be honoured, respected, and listened to
- Pastors and elders are appointed by God to have spiritual authority and give oversight in the church

When it comes to the bigger decisions in life - relocating, getting married, or a major course change in life - it would be wise to invite your church leaders to share their counsel with you.

The Bible tells us that a church leader will be accountable for how they lead you:

> "Obey your leaders and submit to them - for they keep watch over your souls as those who will give an account ..." (Hebrews 13:17, NASB)

This means that their advice is different and weightier than the advice that a friend gives.

Of course, these principles only apply and work if the spiritual leaders over us are leading in a godly way.

What if your husband advises you to make sinful decisions?

What if your parents tell you to stop following Jesus or prohibit you from being baptised?

What if your church leaders are controlling and self-seeking?

God is our ultimate authority and leader. His word, the Bible, is our ultimate guide and source of wisdom. If a husband, a parent, or a church leader advises you to live in a way that is contrary to the Bible, then their advice should not be followed.

Here are some guidelines for pastors and elders when advising church members:

- Pastors and elders should only instruct and direct where the Bible clearly instructs and directs. For example: if an unmarried church member is considering moving in with their unmarried partner, a church leader can direct them not to make this decision as the Bible is clear that sex outside of marriage is a sin.
- In the Catholic church, leaders are called 'priests' which means they are viewed as mediators between God and the people. However, pastors and elders are not to function this way. The New Testament teaches that all believers are priests (see

Revelation 1:6, 1 Peter 2:9), which means that we can all hear God for ourselves. A good church leader doesn't act like a priest but instead helps individuals to hear God for themselves. Leaders are not there to control church members, instead, they are to serve them and help them hear God.

- When giving advice, leaders should be prayerful and sensitive to the Holy Spirit. Sometimes, the Holy Spirit will give a prophetic word or words of wisdom or knowledge. These great gifts are special and can help God's people make great decisions.

WHAT SHOULD I DO IF I HAVE A COMPLAINT AGAINST A CHURCH LEADER?

Jesus taught us not to ignore sin in another person's life. Instead, we are to lovingly challenge them. Rather than talking about them in gossip, we are to talk to *them* in love:

> "If your brother or sister sins, go and point out their fault, just between the two of you. If they listen to you, you have won them over. But if they will not listen, take one or two others along, so that 'every matter may be established by the testimony of two or three witnesses.'" (Matthew 18:15-16, NIV)

But what if your concern relates to a church leader?

Paul took Jesus's advice and applied it to church leaders who were sinning:

> "Do not entertain an accusation against an elder unless it is brought by two or three witnesses. But those elders who are sinning you are to reprove before everyone, so that the others may take warning." (1 Timothy 5:19-20, NIV)

On one hand, Paul is protecting leaders from malicious rumours and gossip - we are not to even "entertain an accusation against an elder". Paul understood that most leaders experience undue criticism. Indeed, one of Satan's tactics is to stir up animosity towards church leaders. So, church leaders are to be honoured, prayed for and protected from gossip.

But this does not mean that church leaders are above reproach. Paul teaches that when there are "two or three [credible] witnesses", then a leader should experience church discipline.

Paul encourages full transparency when it comes to dealing with sinning leaders. Timothy was instructed that "those elders who are sinning you are to reprove before everyone." There are to be no cover-ups. Transparency is vital for healthy churches; transparency helps church members trust the leadership team.

Can a leader who has been sinning continue to lead?

Each situation is different. There is a big difference between a leader who has been denying the sin and then is caught compared with a leader who has humbled themselves and asked for help. There are some sinful behaviours which would permanently disqualify a leader from any future leadership role. In other cases, it might be appropriate for the leader to step back from their duties for a period during which they submit to an agreed restoration process and then move back into a leadership role. Thank God that where there is repentance, there is hope - all sins can be forgiven and all people can experience grace.

Such issues of church discipline and accountability highlight the importance of every local church and leadership team operating under apostolic oversight. Apostles will work with local leadership teams to help guide them through these challenging and sensitive situations.

No one is above oversight. Apostles are to be accountable to other leaders too. In Paul's ministry, we see a great example of genuinely accountable leadership. Firstly, the apostle Paul never functioned alone, he always travelled and ministered with a team of others. Secondly, Paul submitted his life and teaching to other apostles and key leaders. In Galatians, Paul describes how he invited other recognised leaders to hold him accountable (see Galatians 2:1-10). Thirdly, when he publicly challenged the hypocrisy of the apostle Peter, Paul modelled how apostles should be held to account for their actions (see Galatians 2:13-14). Modern-day apostles need to follow Paul's example, functioning not as lone rangers, but as part of a team, and operating under the authority of other apostles and leaders.

CAN WOMEN BE CHURCH LEADERS?

"In essentials, unity; in non-essentials, liberty; in all things, charity." This quote, often attributed to Augustine, shapes our approach to the question of women in leadership. Acknowledging its divisive nature, we aim to look at it biblically, sensitively, and with perspective. While crucial, this topic isn't a primary and essential doctrine like the gospel, Christ's nature, or the inspiration of scripture - truths we would die for. As a secondary matter, it allows space for dialogue and differing applications between Bible-believing Christians.

Having said this we will now aim to give clarity for what we believe within the Go Global family of churches.

Before answering this question, it is important to step back and look at the bigger picture of what the Bible says about men and women.

There are two main theological views when it comes to the role of women in the church, they are:

The complementarian view. This holds that men and women are equal in value but in some areas carry different roles.

The egalitarian view. This holds that men and women are equal in value and can function in the same roles in all areas.

If we are to build our lives and churches on scripture, the question we must ask is not 'Which of these views do we like best,' but rather, 'Which of these views is most aligned with what the Bible teaches?'

While there are extreme versions of both of these perspectives (i.e., male chauvinism or extreme feminism), for most part we see good Christian leaders holding to both views with balance and respect.

Notice that both complementarians and egalitarians agree on men and women being equal in value, a point which the Bible is clear on. At creation, the Bible teaches that both men and women are created equally in God's image:

"So God created mankind in his own image, in the image of God he created them; male and female he created them." (Genesis 1:27, NIV)

And in salvation, we see that men and women are considered equal in their standing before God:

"There is neither Jew nor Greek, there is neither slave nor free man, there is neither male nor female; for you are all one in Christ Jesus." (Galatians 3:28, NASB)

This scripture, and indeed the message of Jesus, was revolutionary, being written at a time when Jews looked down on Greeks, slaves were considered the property of their masters and women were seen as second-class citizens.

So then, can women lead in the church?

Throughout the Bible, we see examples of women being used by God in leadership roles.

Here are some Old Testament examples:

- Deborah, a judge and prophet (see Judges 4)
- Huldah, a prophet (see 2 Kings 22)
- Isaiah's wife, a prophet (see Isaiah 8:3)
- Esther, a queen and deliverer (see the book of Esther)

In the New Testament, there are many examples of women in leadership roles:

- We see women prophets: "Philip the evangelist ... had four virgin daughters who were prophetesses." (Acts 21:8-9, NASB)
- Paul referred to "fellow workers" in his ministry who were women: "I entreat Euodia and I entreat Syntyche to agree in the Lord ... help these women, who have laboured side by side with me in the gospel together with Clement and the rest of my fellow workers ..." (Philippians 4:2-3, ESV)

- Paul refers to Nympha who was a leader of a church: "Give my greetings to the brothers at Laodicea, and to Nympha and the church in her house." (Colossians 4:15, ESV)

Paul concludes the book of Romans by referring to many of the key people he had worked with:

"I commend to you our sister Phoebe, a deacon of the church in Cenchreae. I ask you to receive her in the Lord in a way worthy of his people and to give her any help she may need from you, for she has been the benefactor of many people, including me.

Greet Priscilla and Aquila, my co-workers in Christ Jesus. They risked their lives for me. Not only I but all the churches of the Gentiles are grateful to them. Greet also the church that meets at their house …

Greet Mary, who worked very hard for you.

Greet Andronicus and Junia, my fellow Jews who have been in prison with me. They are outstanding among the apostles …

Greet Tryphena and Tryphosa, those women who work hard in the Lord.

Greet my dear friend Persis, another woman who has worked very hard in the Lord.

Greet Rufus, chosen in the Lord, and his mother, who has been a mother to me, too." (Romans 16, NIV)

From this list in Romans, we observe that:

- Phoebe was a deacon carrying leadership responsibility in a church.
- Priscilla and Aquila led alongside Paul. The fact that Priscilla is mentioned first (both here and in other verses) indicates that she was the main leader with her husband alongside. Priscilla was a Bible teacher and mentor of leaders (see Acts 18:26). They also led a house church.

- Andronicus and Junia (probably a husband and wife) are referred to as being "outstanding among the apostles".

In New Testament times, the wider culture was male-dominated and kept women down. It is therefore astonishing to see the number of women who carried leadership roles in the early church. The Bible and the early church were truly counter-cultural in their time.

The global church was dramatically birthed on the day of Pentecost, as described in Acts chapter two. On that day, Peter explained what was happening by quoting from the prophet, Joel:

> "In the last days, God says, I will pour out my Spirit on all people. Your sons and daughters will prophesy, your young men will see visions, your old men will dream dreams. Even on my servants, both men and women, I will pour out my Spirit in those days, and they will prophesy." (Acts 2:17-18, NIV)

God anoints "sons and daughters … men and women" to ministry and we see this clearly in the New Testament (see examples above) and in our day. As we look back to the 1906 Azusa Street revival, which birthed the modern-day Pentecostal and Charismatic movements, we again see the same pattern of God empowering and releasing both men and women into ministry.

> "I think we need to go back … to a one-eyed black preacher in Azusa Street and realise that Pentecost has a habit of giving a platform to the excluded. The modern-day Pentecostal revival released youths as well as elders, rich men and the sons of slaves, sons and daughters, to prophesy. In one fell swoop, Pentecost released bold, vocal ministry to rich and poor, old and young, male and female, bursting through the dividing walls of gender, age and social class." (Alistair Matheson, Apostolic Churches UK)

The Bible indeed teaches that men and women are equal in value. It is also clear from the examples in scripture that men and women can function in most of the same leadership roles. However, the Bible seems to point to a couple of leadership areas where men and women are to function differently - one is in a marriage and the other is in a local congregation.

Scripture reveals that in marriage, husbands and wives have different God-given roles.

> "Wives, submit yourselves to your own husbands as you do to the Lord. For the husband is the head of the wife as Christ is the head of the church … Husbands, love your wives, just as Christ loved the church and gave himself up for her …" (Ephesians 5:22-23, 25, NIV)

The Bible does not say that men, in general, are to lead women, or that men are the 'head' over women. It teaches specifically in the context of marriage that a husband is "the *head* of the wife". Sadly, this truth has been misunderstood, misused and distorted. Some men have used this scripture to justify them acting like dictators in their own homes. Instead, being the 'head' means leading like Jesus. Jesus's leadership was loving, sacrificial and servant-hearted (see also Matthew 20:25-28). So, husbands are called to lay down their lives for their wives, to serve and to love them unconditionally. If a husband is leading like this, it will be much easier for his wife to happily 'submit' to him. The husband being head in the marriage does not mean that they are to make all the decisions, but it does mean that they are responsible for every decision that is made (see Genesis 3). This same principle of headship in marriage can be seen in 1 Corinthians 11:3-16 and 1 Peter 3:7.

Being under authority as leaders not only keeps us spiritually safe, but also being under authority gives us authority. All leaders, both men and women, should humbly operate under the covering of other leaders. For example, pastors should be accountable to apostolic leaders and apostles should be accountable to other apostles. In addition, for leaders who are married women, their authority in leadership partly comes from them living submitted to their husbands. This also sets a powerful example to other wives in the church.

The other male leadership role as described in the Bible, is the position of an elder (or overseer). Paul writes to Timothy with the qualifications of an elder:

"If anyone aspires to the office of overseer, he desires a noble task. Therefore an overseer must be above reproach, the husband of one wife, sober-minded, self-controlled, respectable, hospitable, able to teach, not a drunkard, not violent but gentle, not quarrelsome, not a lover of money. He must manage his own household well, with all dignity keeping his children submissive, for if someone does not know how to manage his own household, how will he care for God's church?" (1 Timothy 3:5, ESV)

Here, Paul uses the analogy of elders being like spiritual fathers who are to faithfully father their own households as well as God's. Here is how one author explains this:

> "We tend to read the term 'elder' as meaning the same thing as 'leader' does in business, politics or industry. In those spheres, it makes sense for the person - irrespective of their sex - who is most competent to be given the position of CEO, president or manager. But when the Bible describes the role of elders, it doesn't really have our corporate contemporary leadership models in view. Rather, the picture is far more of the church as a family, which is overseen and protected by fathers. These fathers are expected to have certain gifts (for example, being able to teach); but their primary qualification is their godly character as fathers.
>
> This is made especially clear in Paul's first letter to Timothy. Throughout this letter Paul relates the biological family to the family of the church, and the church family to the biological one. This is especially plain in his instruction that a man should only be recognised as an elder if he is a good father of his biological family. All kinds of people (of both sexes) should lead in all kinds of areas of church life and ministry - but only men can be fathers. Women should not be elders because women cannot be fathers. This is not to say that a woman should not lead a business as the CEO or lead a nation as the President or Prime Minister, as those areas of life are not in the same category as a church family. And ... it does not mean that women should not hold extremely significant

positions of leadership in the church. If there are fathers in the church, then there must also be mothers ..." (P. J. Smyth, Elders, p46-47)

So, the Bible seems to point to elders typically being men as it is a fatherly leadership role. While this is true, it is important to recognise that there are some contexts where, by necessity, there is a different outworking of this. For example, in much of the Chinese underground church where most of the leaders are women.

We suggest the dual conviction of male headship in marriage and male eldership in a church should be carried differently, holding the latter less tightly and more pragmatically. The role of a husband in a marriage is non-negotiable as it is an eternal illustration of Christ and His church, and established by God in His creational order. The principle of male eldership in a church should be honoured but with appropriate flexibility based on context and how to best serve each church. In other words, while male eldership seems to be the rule, we are open to there being exceptions to this rule, where godly women carry eldership responsibilities in some situations.

In the Go Global family of churches, we are passionate about releasing women into church leadership. We have great women pastors, preachers, church planters, prophets and deacons. When it comes to eldership, we would typically appoint 'eldership couples' (as opposed to appointing single men) so that the wife can function alongside her husband in the role. Some churches in Go Global have women elders. They are excellent leaders who have our support. We believe churches are to be led by leadership teams with both men and women, which reflect the multifaceted gifts present in the congregation.

In summary:

- Men and women are created with equal value before God.
- We can see from scripture that both men and women can carry prominent leadership roles within the church, indeed Paul celebrates the key women leaders who served alongside him.
- Scripture teaches that in marriage husbands are to be the "head".
- Scripture points to eldership as typically a male role.

This theological view would be described as a soft complementarian perspective.

In closing, let's delve into two contentious sections within Paul's writings that often spark questions regarding the role of women in churches. We'll endeavour to shed light on the interpretation of these passages for better understanding.

> Question: Paul wrote "the women are to keep silent" (1 Corinthians 14:34), how then can women be leaders?
>
> Answer: Paul also wrote in the same book, giving guidelines on how women are to prophesy (see 1 Corinthians 11), something that cannot be done silently. So, it is fair to conclude that he wasn't making a general rule but was addressing a specific situation.
>
> Question: How can women be leaders when Paul stated, "I do not allow a woman to teach or to exercise authority over a man" (1 Timothy 2:12)?
>
> Answer: Paul's "co-worker" Priscilla, with her husband Aquila alongside, took the skilled Bible teacher, Apollos "aside and explained to him the way of God more accurately" (Acts 18:26). She corrected this humble leader in his doctrine and he welcomed it. It is commonly understood that Paul's statement in 1 Timothy 2 was either addressing women who were disrupting the church or women who were assuming the role of eldership.

DIDN'T THE ROLE OF APOSTLES PASS AWAY AFTER THE FIRST GENERATION OF APOSTLES DIED?

Some argue there were only 13 apostles (the twelve plus Paul) and that after they passed away, so too did the gift of apostolic ministry in the church. Those who hold this belief would typically say that one of the qualifications of an apostle was that they had personally seen the risen Jesus (see 1 Corinthians 9:1). Their view is linked to the belief that it was the apostles alone who were authorised to write scripture and since the canon of scripture is now complete, there are no longer any apostles. It is worth considering each of these points in order.

Firstly, as we have detailed in Study 5, the New Testament records that there were far more than 13 apostles.

In Revelation 2:2, as Jesus congratulates the Ephesus church for its discernment, He says: "you have tested those who claim to be apostles but are not, and have found them false." If there were only thirteen apostles in the early church, there would be no need to 'test' those who claimed to have apostolic ministry. In every age, Satan will try to infiltrate God's people with false leaders - fake apostles, prophets, evangelists, pastors and teachers. The existence of counterfeits points to the presence of the true leadership gifts that God continues to give to the church.

Was seeing the risen Jesus really a qualification for apostolic ministry? Beyond the original 13, there is no record of the other apostles listed in the New Testament, as having seen the risen Jesus and yet the New Testament refers to them as apostles.

While it is true that some of the original 13 apostles wrote books in the New Testament, it is worth noting that, not all of them wrote scripture and Luke, a non-apostle, wrote two of the books (Luke and Acts).

The belief that the apostles have passed away is not only untrue but it's actually unhelpful and undermining to the church in our generation. This brings us to the most important reason why we believe in modern-day apostles. Ephesians chapter four tells us the reason why these ministries have been given:

> "He gave some as apostles, some as prophets, some as evangelists, some as pastors and teachers, for the equipping of the saints for the work of ministry, for the building up of the body of Christ; until we all attain to the unity of the faith, and of the knowledge of the Son of God, to a mature man, to the measure of the stature which belongs to the fullness of Christ." (Ephesians 4:11-13, NASB)

It takes all of these ministries to fully equip the saints for the work of ministry. Without apostolic input, the provision would be lopsided. It is also clear that these ministries are given to the church "until we all attain to the unity of the faith". I don't know anyone who would dare claim that the church is fully mature and united! Jesus will be returning for a glorious and mature church (see Revelation 19:7), and these ministries are an essential part of His strategy to prepare the church for His return.

Having said this, it is important to clarify that modern-day apostles should not be viewed as having the same authority as the original 12 plus Paul. The original 13 played a unique role in history as eyewitnesses to the resurrection, writing scripture and setting the course of the church for the ages to come. As some people describe it, apostles today should be considered as small 'a' apostles.

A UNITED, LOVING AND CHARISMATIC COMMUNITY

"Those who accepted his message were baptised, and about three thousand were added to their number that day. They devoted themselves to the apostles' teaching and to fellowship, to the breaking of bread and to prayer. Everyone was filled with awe at the many wonders and signs performed by the apostles. All the believers were together and had everything in common. They sold property and possessions to give to anyone who had need. Every day they continued to meet together in the temple courts. They broke bread in their homes and ate together with glad and sincere hearts, praising God and enjoying the favour of all the people. And the Lord added to their number daily those who were being saved." (Acts 2:41-47, NIV)

On the day of Pentecost, after the Holy Spirit was poured out and Peter preached to the vast gathered crowd, we are told that 3,000 people were saved and added to the church. What follows, as recounted in the passage above, is one of the most beautiful descriptions of community.

Many wrongly assume that a large growing church isn't welcoming and lacks depth of community. The Jerusalem church dispels this myth. From day one, it had more than 3,000 members and yet it was neither impersonal nor shallow. People debate which is best, the mega-church or the house church? The answer is both! Quantity and quality are not necessarily mutually exclusive. With God's help and wise leadership, both are achievable.

The church was both big and small. It had many people and regular big gatherings in the temple courts, an area able to accommodate crowds of thousands. Yet it was small, with believers enjoying close relationships and community in their homes. As believers, we need both the big and the small. The big gathering with worship and preaching inspires our faith and vision. Whilst the small gatherings meet our need to be known and for accountability.

In this study, we will look specifically at three aspects of the early church which we aspire to reflect in our church communities today.

A UNITED CHURCH

> "They devoted themselves to the apostles' teaching and to **fellowship**, to the breaking of bread and to prayer." (Acts 2:42, NIV)

The word 'fellowship' in Greek is the word 'koinōnia'. It means a deep connection with others based on something shared in common.

In life, we all experience community in such a way. For example, if you were to join a football team because you love the game, it won't be long before you experience community in the team. The community is a by-product and comes out of a shared passion for a sport.

People experience community based on shared hobbies, ethnicities, professions, financial status or political affiliation.

What's unique in Acts 2 is the fact that people were experiencing deep fellowship, yet they were coming from hugely different social classes (see Acts 2:45) and ethnicities (see Acts 2:5). They were experiencing unity amid diversity.

The foundation for Christian unity is our shared experience of being saved by Jesus and being part of the family of God. We are united in the knowledge that our sins are forgiven, we've been filled with His Spirit, we're on a mission together and heaven-bound. This is more important than any earthly allegiance.

Our unity doesn't come from focusing on community; it comes by focusing on Jesus, the One we share in common.

"Has it ever occurred to you that one hundred pianos all tuned to the same fork are automatically tuned to each other? They are of one accord by being tuned, not to each other, but to another standard to which each one must individually bow. So, one hundred worshipers [meeting] together, each one looking away to Christ, are in heart nearer to each other than they could possibly be, were they to become 'unity' conscious and turn their eyes away from God to strive for closer fellowship." (A. W. Tozer, The Pursuit of God)

Some may seek to achieve unity by watering the truth down so as not to offend anyone. However, this isn't the kind of unity we see in scripture. The opposite is true. We unite around the greatest and strongest truths, such as salvation found in Jesus alone, the Bible as God's word and the mission of sharing the gospel with our generation.

"When the Bible speaks about church unity, it speaks of unity not at the expense of truth but on the basis of it." (John Blanchard)

Unity is a powerful thing. In Psalm 133, we read that God pours out blessings on His people who are united:

"How good and pleasant it is when God's people live together in unity… For there the Lord bestows his blessing, even life forevermore." (Psalm 133:1, 3, NIV)

Jesus, in His prayer before His arrest, known as the High Priestly Prayer, revealed that when the church is united, then the world will start believing in Him.

"I pray also for those who will believe in me through their message, that all of them may be one, Father, just as you are in me and I am in you. May they also be in us so that the world may believe that you have sent me. I have given them the glory that you gave me, that they may be one as we are one— I in them and you in me—so that they may be brought to complete unity. Then the world will know that you sent me and have loved them even as you have loved me." (John 17:20-23, NIV)

In light of this, it's no surprise that the church in Jerusalem experienced such great growth and blessing. We read: "And the Lord added to their number daily those who were being saved." (Acts 2:47)

Our generation needs to see such a move of God through the church. We long to see God adding to our "number daily those who" are "being saved". We are therefore committed to protecting the unity of God's people, both within the local church community and between churches.

A LOVING CHURCH

One of the things that stands out in the church community described in Acts 2 is their radical generosity. We read:

"All the believers were together and had everything in common. They sold property and possessions to give to anyone who had need." (Acts 2:44-45)

In His parable, the Sheep and the Goats, Jesus made it clear that you'd be able to identify God's people by the way they generously share their time, their food and drink, their property and their concern. Jesus revealed that He takes personally how we treat others in the church:

"...whatever you did for one of the least of these brothers of mine, you did for me." (Matthew 25:39, NIV)

It's amazing to think that by loving the church you're loving Jesus.

Believers are called by God to love all people, both those inside and those outside of the church. When we love those outside the church, we're loving and valuing people created in God's image. But when we love those inside the church, we're loving those who are in God's family. This is our starting point – when we love the people in the church family, this love spills out into the world.

> "...as we have opportunity, let us do good to all people, especially to those who belong to the family of believers." (Galatians 6:10, NIV)

Our love has got to go beyond feelings and words; we are to love others with actions.

> "...let's not merely say that we love each other; let us show the truth by our actions." (1 John 3:18, NLT)

Just as the church is made up of people who are different from each other, so Scripture challenges us to get out of our comfort zones and actively love those not like us.

> Jesus said: "If you love those who love you, what credit is that to you? Even sinners love those who love them." (Luke 6:32-36, NIV)

The apostle James strongly challenges us:

> "My brothers and sisters, believers in our glorious Lord Jesus Christ must not show favouritism. Suppose a man comes into your meeting wearing a gold ring and fine clothes, and a poor man in filthy old clothes also comes in. If you show special attention to the man wearing fine clothes and say, "Here's a good seat for you," but say to the poor man, "You stand there" or "Sit on the floor by my feet," have you not discriminated among yourselves and become judges with evil thoughts?" (James 2:1-4, NIV)

Reading Acts chapter 2, you'd be tempted to think that the early church was a perfect spiritual utopia where no one was offended, and where no one felt let down or hurt. But alas this was not the case. In later chapters in Acts, we see hypocrisy creeping into the Jerusalem church (see Acts 5:1-11) and racial tensions emerging (see Acts 6:1). In fact, as you go through the whole book of Acts, you'll see many great churches emerging, which, like the church in Jerusalem, were full of life, love and power. However, as you read the letters Paul and the other apostles wrote to these churches later in the New Testament, you discover there really was no perfect church, only a perfect Saviour. You'll be disillusioned very quickly with the church if you have a wrong illusion in the first place.

So, the challenge we are all faced with is the very real challenge of loving people who are imperfect, of loving people who will let us down, who may offend us or even hurt us. But this is where we learn the greatest lesson - we learn to love like God loves. He loves and is committed to imperfect people, and He commands us:

> "A new command I give you: Love one another. As I have loved you, so you must love one another." (John 13:34, NIV)

Too many believers run from this sort of gritty love. So many will move churches or stop connecting entirely when they are offended, let down or faced with hypocrisy. But in doing so, they miss out on what God wanted to do in their lives. Technically, you can be a Christian without going to church, but you can't live the Christian life without the church. There is a work that God does in our souls which can only happen in the context of the local church. He uses even the rough edges of others to change you, sanctify you and make you more like Jesus. So, let's love like Jesus loves. Don't quit on church because Jesus doesn't quit on the church, His Bride. Don't pull the church down because Jesus said He's building it up (see Matthew 16:18). Just as we want others to have grace for us and our imperfections, so too let's have grace for others.

A CHARISMATIC CHURCH

In Acts chapter 2, we read that the church was birthed with the outpouring of the Holy Spirit at Pentecost. As we journey through the pages of Acts, we see that the church continued to grow as the Holy Spirit worked in it.

In 1 Corinthians chapters 12-14, we discover that God gives nine supernatural gifts of the Holy Spirit to His church, and these gifts should be seen and experienced when the church gathers together.

> "Now to each one the manifestation of the Spirit is given for the common good. To one there is given through the Spirit a message of wisdom, to another a message of knowledge by means of the same Spirit, to another faith by the same Spirit, to another gifts of healing by that one Spirit, to another miraculous powers, to another prophecy, to another distinguishing between spirits, to another speaking in different kinds of tongues, and to still another the interpretation of tongues. All these are the work of one and the same Spirit, and he distributes them to each one, just as he determines." (1 Corinthians 12:7-11, NIV)

There is an expectation that when the church meets, the Holy Spirit will distribute these gifts for people to share and encourage those gathered.

> "When you come together, each of you has a hymn, or a word of instruction, a revelation, a tongue or an interpretation. Everything must be done so that the church may be built up." (1 Corinthians 14:26, NIV)

Our church, like many others, believes in and practises operating in the gifts of the Holy Spirit. This kind of church is known as a 'charismatic church'. This comes from the Greek word for 'gifts' which is 'charismata', meaning 'a gift of grace'. A gift of grace means it wasn't earned by good behaviour or spiritual maturity. Some people wrongly believe that people who operate in these gifts are somehow in a class of their own, that they are spiritual giants, living perfect lives. The good news is that God makes these gifts available to all His people. It's all by grace (see Galatians 3:5).

The book of Corinthians offers several guidelines relating to the gifts of the Spirit:

- When operating in the gifts of the Holy Spirit, make sure you are motivated by love for the people, rather than making yourself look good (see 1 Corinthians 13:1-3).
- Even though these gifts are available, God expects us to "earnestly desire" them. Typically, God will give out these gifts in response to us asking Him for them (see 1 Corinthians 14:1).
- Make sure you are wise and credible in the way you operate in these gifts in a public gathering so that you don't put off visitors or unbelievers with unnecessary jargon or behaviour (see 1 Corinthians 14:23-25).
- All words and prophecies should be checked with scripture (see 1 Corinthians 14:29).

We encourage all believers to learn to operate in these gifts. For practical reasons, in bigger gatherings, we typically encourage leaders to operate in the gifts. In smaller gatherings, we encourage every believer to step out and "earnestly desire" the gifts, bringing encouragement to each other.

Just as the early church grew in depth and number by being united, by radically loving and by flowing in the gifts of the Holy Spirit, so, let's commit to seeing these hallmarks in our churches today.

BEING A UNITED, LOVING AND CHARISMATIC COMMUNITY TODAY

Be united and loving

There is great power in a united and loving church. Unfortunately, our enemy, the devil, also knows this. Satan will do everything he can to undermine unity within a church and unity between churches. He does this in two ways:

- The devil will trap people with feelings of bitterness towards others in the church.

   "See to it that no one falls short of the grace of God and that no bitter root grows up to cause trouble and defile many." (Hebrews 12:15, NIV)

Bitterness not only ruins the life of the person who is carrying it, it also negatively impacts those around them in church.

- The devil will entice people to gossip about and slander others in the church.

This is no surprise as he is called the accuser and the slanderer. Sometimes what starts as a legitimate concern soon becomes bitterness, which in time becomes slander and gossip. The Bible teaches that "… one who spreads strife among brothers" (Proverbs 6:19, NASB) is an "abomination" to God!

In light of these demonic strategies, let's "make every effort to keep the unity of the Spirit through the bond of peace." (Ephesians 4:3, NIV)

Commit to walk in forgiveness with others, not allowing bitterness to build up in your soul. If you have a problem with someone in the church, go and talk to them:

"If your brother or sister sins, go and point out their fault, just between the two of you." (Matthew 18:15, NIV)

If you believe someone in the church has a problem with you, go and talk to them!

"Therefore, if you are offering your gift at the altar and there remember that your brother or sister has something against you, leave your gift there in front of the altar. First go and be reconciled to them; then come and offer your gift." (Matthew 5:23-24, NIV)

Make a decision not to gossip or slander others. Make a decision not to even associate with those who do, as scripture says:

"…do not associate with a gossip." (Proverbs 20:19, NASB)

Be in a small group

As we learned earlier, the early church met in big and small gatherings. The small group or home group gathering is so important for your spiritual growth.

In Russia, when the Communists came to power in 1917 under Lenin, they removed several prominent church leaders. The church in Russia was hugely affected because the church system was built around leaders and gatherings. However, in China, because of the home group discipleship movement, when communism rose under Mao in 1949, Christianity didn't die. Church leaders knew how to make disciples in small groups. House churches flourished and nationally, the church grew to more than 100 million believers during the communist era.

> "New Christians who connect with a small group are five more times likely to be active in the church five years later than those who attend only worship services." (Bob Whitesel)

Lifeway Research surveyed 3000 churches and discovered:

- 67% of small group attendees read their Bible regularly compared to 27% among non-small group attendees.
- 64% of small group attendees pray for church and leaders regularly compared to 30% of non-small group attendees.
- 79% of small group attendees confess sins and ask forgiveness compared to 54% of non-small group attendees.

Jesus started His ministry by gathering a small group of disciples.

So, commit to connect with a small group.

And don't just attend a small group - love the people in that small group and be like a family. In this environment, your faith will grow.

Be charismatic

> "Follow the way of love and eagerly desire gifts of the Spirit, especially prophecy." (1 Corinthians 14:1, NIV)

Don't be passive when it comes to the gifts of the Holy Spirit. Let's be people who "earnestly desire" the gifts. Operating in the gifts of the Spirit is one of the ways we express love to others within the church family. You might be carrying the word of encouragement that they need to hear.

FREQUENTLY ASKED QUESTIONS

HOW DO I KNOW WHAT MY SPIRITUAL GIFT IS?

Because you have the Holy Spirit, you have the opportunity to operate in all His gifts, but some gifts will be more emphasised in you than others. Let's explore this in more detail.

1 Corinthians 12:7-11 lists the nine gifts that the Holy Spirit gives. The ultimate gift, however, is the Holy Spirit Himself. Jesus referred to the Holy Spirit as "the gift my Father promised" (Acts 1:4). All believers are privileged to be given the gift of the Holy Spirit and if we have the Holy Spirit, we have Him who has all the other nine gifts. We therefore believe that all of God's children have access to all the gifts because we all have the Holy Spirit residing in our lives. This means we can all expect to prophesise, see miracles, speak in tongues and get words of knowledge (see Mark 16:17-18).

Having said that, all the gifts are available to all of us, it seems that God will work through us all differently in the context of the gathered church. In 1 Corinthians 12:28-32, we are told that "in the church" we will not all flow in the same gifts. It is evident that God will tend to cause specific people to operate with specific gifts. We can see examples of this in church life. There are some people whom God uses to see healings and miracles as they pray for the sick. Others commonly receive prophetic visions, dreams or pictures. Some flow powerfully in words of knowledge revealing truths about people's lives that only God could have known. Others bring inspired messages in tongues with interpretation so everyone can understand. Sometimes, the spiritual gifts we flow in are linked to our natural gifts. For example, people who are natural encouragers can often flow in the spiritual gift of prophecy. Or people who are excellent counsellors may find that God gives them words of wisdom. Just as God has created us differently, so too He works through us all differently.

For each of us therefore we should first and foremost be grateful for the presence of the Holy Spirit in our lives and then "eagerly desire gifts of the Spirit" (1 Corinthians 14:1). We first appreciate the Giver and then the gifts He gives. Before going to a church gathering try asking God to give you something for someone in the church. As you do this, He will give you His gifts. In time, and with experience, you will start to recognise the gifts in which you flow.

IS IT EVER RIGHT TO MOVE CHURCH?

There are good reasons and bad reasons to consider moving between churches.

Here are some bad reasons people move churches:

- They think the worship music is better in the other church.
- The other church has a nicer building.
- There is more chance of finding a spouse in the other church.
- They were offended or hurt and instead of working to resolve the issue they simply moved churches.
- A leader challenged them on their sinful lifestyle and instead of repenting they simply moved to another church where they are not known.

It is quite common for people who are moving church for such wrong or shallow reasons to pretend their decision is purely spiritual. The words, "The Lord is leading me to move on", are usually not far from their lips.

Moving between churches for the wrong reasons shows a lack of respect for His Church and also hinders people from maturing in their faith. Imagine uprooting a tree and relocating it into new soil every few months. The tree would never grow to reach its full potential. As a rule, it is good to stay 'planted' in the church that God has placed you in. As the psalmist wrote, "planted in the house of the Lord, they will flourish in the courts of our God" (Psalm 92:13).

When Paul wrote letters to congregations, he would frequently open by addressing them to the church in a particular city. For example, "To the church of God in Corinth ..." (1 Corinthians 1:2). If we received such a letter today, we might well ask, which church? Corinth Baptist Church, Corinth Presbyterian Church, or The Corinth Charismatic Fellowship? The fact that Paul began letters this way seems to indicate that each city or town had one church or at least one unified leadership. When writing to churches in a region - for example, "To the churches in Galatia ..." (Galatians 1:2) - it is clear that Paul assumes there to be close ties and good communication between churches and leaders.

Two thousand years later, the church in today's world is more complicated. There is a variety of different denominations and expressions in most localities. Despite this, we believe there can still be truth-based unity between churches and church leaders. Indeed, Jesus prayed it would be so (see John 17:21).

In New Testament times, the idea of moving to a different church was not even a consideration - there were no other churches! Instead of moving every time they were offended, the early believers would have to stay and work things out, and, in doing so, grew in maturity.

As a rule, it is right to stay 'planted' and remain loyal to your church. However, there are moments when it's appropriate for someone to consider moving on.

Sometimes it is right to move because something is unhealthy in the church. For example:

- If the church has moved away from teaching the Bible and is watering down truth.
- If the church is no longer open to the Holy Spirit moving among them.
- If the leadership culture is self-serving and domineering rather than servant-hearted and empowering.

There are other occasions when it is right to move churches, not because there is anything wrong with your old church, but simply because God is genuinely leading you to move. For example:

- You can see that the mission and vision of another church are very similar to the vision God has given you.
- You can see that the gift God has given you could help serve another church.

When considering moving churches for these right reasons, we would encourage you to not just announce your decision to your leaders but instead involve them in the process. This not only protects you from acting unaccountably and making a wrong choice, but it also honours the leaders God has placed in your life (see Hebrews 13:17). How you go about making your decision is just as important as what your decision eventually is.

We would also encourage church leaders to talk to other church leaders. If someone has left another church to come to your church, it is important to honour the other church by talking to the leaders there. This open, transparent and sometimes tough conversation between leaders strengthens genuine unity between churches.

If a leader discovers that someone has left another church for the wrong reasons, they must do what they can to resolve the situation. In some cases, this may mean that they end up going back to their old church, having resolved the issue.

BEING DISCIPLES WHO MAKE DISCIPLES

Having accomplished salvation for us by His death on the cross and His resurrection, Jesus goes on to commission His disciples before ascending back to heaven.

> "Then Jesus came to them and said, "All authority in heaven and on earth has been given to me. Therefore go and make disciples of all nations, baptising them in the name of the Father and of the Son and of the Holy Spirit, and teaching them to obey everything I have commanded you. And surely I am with you always, to the very end of the age." (Matthew 28:18-20, NIV)

This has become known as the 'Great Commission' and continues to be the mission of the church in every generation, till His return and the "end of the age". In this study, we will first unpack what it means to be a disciple and then look at how to make disciples.

WHAT IS A DISCIPLE?

When Jesus called His first disciples, the fishermen, Peter and Andrew, He declared:

"Follow Me, and I will make you fishers of people." (Matthew 4:19, NASB)

In this statement, we see the three essential characteristics of a disciple:

"Follow Me"

A disciple is a person who is following Jesus.

Many people in the church think they are following Jesus, but the reality is they just want Jesus to follow them! They like the idea of having Jesus in their lives but want Him to bless their decisions, serve their purposes and do their will.

It was common in Jesus' time for Jewish rabbis to have disciples who followed and learned from them. Indeed, in every generation, people tend to follow others they admire, whether it's political leaders, sporting heroes or celebrities.

Jesus, however, stands out from all other leaders. Firstly, Jesus is not just a man, He's fully man and fully God. Secondly, as an act of sacrificial love, He laid down His life to save us. Thirdly, He conquered death and today is seated at the right hand of God and one day we're told that:

"... at the name of Jesus every knee will bow, of those who are in heaven and on earth and under the earth, and that every tongue will confess that Jesus Christ is Lord ..." (Philippians 2:10-11, NASB)

So, following Jesus isn't just a nice religious idea, it's eternally appropriate and essential.

The word 'disciple' in Greek is 'mathetes' which means 'a follower' or 'a learner'. So, a disciple of Jesus is someone who, having been saved by grace, now embarks on a lifelong journey of submitting to, learning from and seeking to become like Jesus.

Some 27 times in the New Testament, people like us are called "believers", five times they are called "followers", three times they are called "Christians," but more than 269 times, believers were called "disciples".

It is impossible to be a true believer or a Christian unless you are also a disciple. Being a disciple means not only a belief in Jesus but also a humble submission to Him as Lord and leader of your life. As Paul writes:

> "If you declare with your mouth, "Jesus is Lord," and believe in your heart that God raised him from the dead, you will be saved." (Romans 10:9, NIV)

Being a disciple means you happily submit to Him as Lord out of love for and faith in Jesus and actively seek to please Him in all areas of your life. It is that simple. Jesus leads; we follow.

For the avoidance of any doubt, living as a disciple of Jesus isn't a means of earning God's approval and acceptance. Rather, it's His unconditional approval and acceptance that fuels your desire to live as a lifelong disciple. You are saved by His work for you, not your work for Him.

"And I will make you"

A disciple is someone who is being changed by Jesus.

Once you become a follower of Jesus, He starts to change you into the ideal version of you. Discipleship involves Jesus moulding our hearts to become more like Him. Paul describes this in Romans and Corinthians:

> "For those God foreknew he also predestined to be conformed to the image of his Son ..." (Romans 8:29, NIV)

> "And the Lord - who is the Spirit - makes us more and more like him as we are changed into his glorious image." (2 Corinthians 3:18, NLT)

Jesus doesn't invite perfect people to follow Him. In fact, in the gospels, we can see the rough edges of all the disciples. Peter was brash, James and John were judgmental, and Matthew was a corrupt tax collector. Jesus didn't choose His followers based on who they were, He chose them, knowing who they would become. Becoming like Jesus is an ongoing process without an endpoint on this side of eternity.

What does becoming more like Jesus look like?

At the Last Supper, Jesus dramatically demonstrated His love for the disciples by assuming the place of a household servant and humbly washing their feet. He then went on to exhort them:

> "You call me 'Teacher' and 'Lord,' and rightly so, for that is what I am. Now that I, your Lord and Teacher, have washed your feet, you also should wash one another's feet. I have set you an example that you should do as I have done for you." (John 13:13-15, NIV)

He then followed up with an instruction:

> "A new command I give you: Love one another. As I have loved you, so you must love one another." (John 13:34, NIV)

Becoming more like Jesus means loving and serving people both within God's household and those outside the church.

You may ask, given that Jesus was fully God while also being fully man, is becoming more like Him, not an impossible goal? In your strength it is impossible, but with God's Spirit working in us, change is possible.

William Temple, the Archbishop of Canterbury in the 1940s, writes:

> "It is no good giving me a play like Hamlet or King Lear, and telling me to write a play like that. Shakespeare could do it — I can't. And it is no good showing me a life like the life of Jesus and telling me to live a life like that. Jesus could do it — I can't. But if the genius of Shakespeare could come and live in me, then I could write plays like this. And if the Spirit of Jesus could come and live in me, then I could live a life like his."

Following Jesus isn't about following a set of ancient instructions like a cold, emotionless robot, rather it's a relationship with Jesus who is alive. Being a disciple is an adventure. The first disciples followed Jesus physically because He was with them in person; today, we follow Jesus who is with us by His Spirit (see John 14:17-20). Just as Jesus said: "And surely I am with you always, to the very end of the age." (Matthew 28:20,

NIV). God doesn't expect us to love and serve others in our strength, instead, we are to partner with the Holy Spirit and allow the love and power of God to flow through our actions and words. As Peter writes:

> "If anyone serves, they should do so with the strength God provides ..."
> (1 Peter 4:11, NIV)

God's purpose is to make us like Jesus, and God's way is to fill us with his Holy Spirit.

"Fishers of people"

A disciple is a person who is committed to Jesus' mission to make other disciples.

> "Jesus said ... As the Father has sent me, I am sending you." (John 20:21, NIV)

Just as Jesus came into the world to reach people and make disciples, in the same way, disciples are called to make disciples. A disciple is someone who partners with God and embraces Jesus's mission to reach the world.

Our mission is not simply to come to church each Sunday, to be nice to other people, or to cram a lot of knowledge about the Bible into our heads. It's not even to give money to the church so that the leaders can carry out the mission of Jesus. It's for every disciple to join in God's mission.

In summary, what is a disciple? A disciple is a person:

- Who is following Jesus.
- Who is being changed by Jesus.
- Who is committed to the mission of Jesus.

This now leads us to our next question ...

HOW DO WE MAKE DISCIPLES?

> "… go and make disciples of all nations, baptising them in the name of the Father and of the Son and of the Holy Spirit, and teaching them to obey everything I have commanded you. And surely I am with you always, to the very end of the age." (Matthew 28:19-20, NIV)

Here, Jesus gives the church its mission, one that will continue until His return. In the same way that Jesus made disciples, so we are now to "make disciples". Just as discipleship is a journey, so too making disciples is a journey with several steps.

Engage

Many Christians view discipleship solely as a process by which believers become stronger believers. In other words, they view discipleship as a "members-only" experience. But when Jesus commissioned His disciples to "make disciples of all nations" they didn't think for a moment that they were to find some believers and make them into better believers - there were no believers then. The early disciples knew that Jesus was calling them to introduce those within the Roman Empire and beyond to Jesus and His saving work. They were to call people to believe, to repent of sin and become followers of Jesus, just as they had.

The starting point of discipleship is evangelism. We are to share the gospel and invite people to follow Jesus. As Jesus said to His first disciples:

> "Follow Me, and I will make you become fishers of men." (Mark 1:17, NASB)

While not everyone is called to be an evangelist (see Ephesians 4:11), every believer is called to evangelise.

How do we evangelise? We are to follow Jesus' example. Jesus was deliberately friends with people who were far from God, so much so that His critics called Him "a friend of tax collectors and sinners" (Matthew 11:19).

The Gospels record for us 132 encounters that Jesus had with individuals. They happened in a variety of locations:

- 6 were in the Temple
- 4 in the synagogues
- But 122 were on streets, at people's houses, at parties, beside wells, at weddings, under trees ... etc.

It's clear that Jesus did not expect people, especially nonbelievers, to jump into His world, so He jumped into theirs. He understood that holiness is separation from sin, not separation from sinners. He walked where they walked, but He did not do what they did. He spent time with drunkards but never got drunk. He was with corrupt tax officials, but He was not corrupt. He extended compassion to prostitutes but never compromised His moral standards.

Today, Jesus, by His Spirit, still wants to be a "friend of sinners", He wants you and I to be His arms and legs, to be His mouthpiece.

We're all called to make disciples, which means we're all called to share the gospel and introduce others to Jesus.

Establish

Having told us to "go and make disciples", Jesus then went on to explain how we are to help establish disciples in their new faith. He said: "Baptising them in the name of the Father and of the Son and of the Holy Spirit, and teaching them to obey everything I have commanded you."

We now come back full circle to the verses we started these studies with. Jesus showed that His words and teachings are foundations for our lives:

"... everyone who hears these words of mine and puts them into practice is like a wise man who built his house on the rock. The rain came down, the streams rose, and the winds blew and beat against that house; yet it did not fall, because it had its foundation on the rock. But everyone who hears these words of mine and does not put them into practice is like a foolish man who built his house on sand. The rain came down, the streams rose, and the winds blew and beat against that house, and it fell with a great crash." (Matthew 7:24-27, NIV)

When someone becomes a believer - a disciple - they've been rescued from Satan's Kingdom and brought into God's Kingdom (see Colossians 1:13), and the devil's not happy! That's why in these early stages of a person's journey with God it's common for them to face storms and temptations, which are designed to make them give up (see Matthew 13:21).

Knowing that storms are coming, seasoned disciples are to help new disciples live by God's word, thus establishing them on a solid, storm-resistant foundation.

Who is responsible for putting these foundations in place? While church leaders will certainly help, it is also the responsibility of all God's people to help new disciples. Very simply, if your friend comes to faith in Jesus, then you should take them under your wing and help them to grow.

What are some essential foundations that new disciples need to be established?

- They need to be baptised.
- They need to start the habit of reading the Bible (it is best if they begin with a gospel and Acts).
- They need to be baptised with the Holy Spirit.
- They need to be connected in a church community.

Who can baptise a new believer? If you are a disciple, you are not only allowed to baptise, you've also been commissioned by Jesus to make disciples and baptise "them in the name of the Father and of the Son and of the Holy Spirit." Find some water deep enough to fully immerse them and go for it.

Equip

Being a disciple is a lifelong journey of learning and becoming like Jesus. Having been established on good foundations, the next part of our discipleship journey is to grow and be equipped. God has deliberately placed a variety of leadership gifts in the church to equip us and help us mature - that's why being fully connected to the life of a church is essential for your growth as a disciple. We return to the Ephesians 4 passage, which we also looked at in Study 5:

> "And He gave some as apostles, some as prophets, some as evangelists, some as pastors and teachers, for the equipping of the saints for the work of ministry, for the building up of the body of Christ; until we all attain to the unity of the faith, and of the knowledge of the Son of God, to a mature man, to the measure of the stature which belongs to the fullness of Christ." (Ephesians 4:11-13, NASB)

These five leadership gifts are there to equip God's people in the work of ministry, or as the New Living Translation puts it: "Their responsibility is to equip God's people to do His work". It's vital to notice that the purpose of being equipped isn't merely to know more things. Rather, it's that you can "do His work" or do "the work of ministry." Information isn't the goal; mobilisation of God's people is.

Each person in a different form of leadership will equip you differently:

- Apostles will equip you with apostolic vision and strategy.
- Prophets will equip you to hear God and sense His leading.
- Evangelists will equip you with a passion for souls and wisdom to effectively reach people.
- Pastors will equip you to care deeply for God's people.
- Teachers will equip you with the ability to grasp the truth and to be able to teach others.

Some leaders make the mistake of waiting for disciples to reach a certain level of maturity before they allow them to do God's work. But in Ephesians 4, it's evident that our maturity (Ephesians 4:13) comes out of us doing the "work of ministry" (Ephesians 4:12). We grow as disciples by getting involved in His work. Rather than waiting for maturity to initiate our ministry, our maturity blossoms through engaging in ministry itself. We grow as we go.

Once a person has come to Christ through the gospel, has become established with good foundations in place, and has grown by being equipped, now they are also commissioned to go and engage others with the gospel. They are, as Jesus said, to "go and make disciples". We are to be disciples who make disciples, who in turn make disciples.

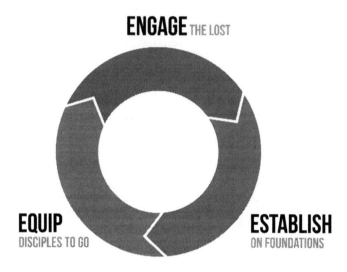

ENGAGE THE LOST

EQUIP
DISCIPLES TO GO

ESTABLISH
ON FOUNDATIONS

An example of this cyclical discipleship journey can be seen in the revival that took place in the ancient city of Ephesus. Firstly, a Christian called Apollos came and **engaged** many in the city with the gospel:

> "... a Jew named Apollos, a native of Alexandria, came to Ephesus ... he spoke with great fervour and taught about Jesus accurately ..." (Acts 18:24-25, NIV)

Following Apollos' visit, the apostle Paul arrived in the city and helped **establish** a number of the new believers by baptising them and praying for them to be filled with the Holy Spirit (see Acts 19:1-6). Paul then proceeded to intensionally teach and **equip** the disciples for ministry:

> "He took the disciples with him and had discussions daily in the lecture hall of Tyrannus. This went on for two years, so that all the Jews and

Greeks who lived in the province of Asia heard the word of the Lord."
(Acts 19:9-10, NIV)

It is evident that the disciples weren't just learning information from Paul, but rather they were going out and in turn, making disciples in the surrounding "province of Asia." They were disciples who were now making disciples. It is believed that as disciples went out from this revival in Ephesus many churches were established in the towns of Colossae, Hierapolis and Laodicea (see Colossians 2:1; 4:13), and possibly also in Smyrna, Pergamum, Thyatira, Sardis and Philadelphia (see Revelation 2:8, 2:12, 2:18, 3:1 3:7).

LOVE - THE ESSENTIAL INGREDIENT FOR EFFECTIVE DISCIPLESHIP

At some point in our growing up, we all learned what might be euphemistically called, the 'facts of life' or the 'birds and the bees'. It may have been through an awkward conversation with a parent, or from friends at school. Either way, we now understand how babies are made, how they are nurtured in those early days, how they grow into maturity and how as adults they can now reproduce and have more babies. But knowing the facts of life alone won't guarantee that you can raise a successful and thriving human being. Why? Because there's also a God-appointed context into which a child should be born and raised - a loving and secure family.

In the same way, discipleship is never to be a mechanical process by which we grow churches. "Making disciples" only works in the healthy context of genuine love, authentic relationships and community.

We share the gospel with others because we love them and are concerned for their eternal well-being. We take time to meet and encourage a new believer because we want them to be grounded in truth ready for any storm. We grow through being equipped and trained for ministry, not so we can boast of what we know, but because now we can better express God's love to others by our actions. We get out of our comfort zones to "go and make disciples" because we know Jesus in His love left heaven's comforts to save and reach us.

Jesus made disciples by spending quality time with twelve young men. He ate with, travelled with, challenged, encouraged, and commissioned them. Ultimately, He loved them, and they knew it.

The great apostle Paul made disciples by always doing life with others. You never see Paul travelling alone, he was always with a team. This team was his disciples, who in time became great apostles, pastors and leaders in their own right.

With this in mind, the best context for you to make disciples and to grow as a disciple is with a small group of other believers - an environment where you can learn, grow and love. So, we encourage churches to intentionally create small group discipleship environments to complement their larger worship gatherings.

The context for effective discipleship is love.

COMMITTING TO THE GREAT COMMISSION

To be disciples who make disciples, there are three commitments we all need to make:

Commit to following Jesus with a small group of others who follow Jesus

Jesus had a small group of disciples, and Paul had a small group of disciples. The best environment for you to grow as a disciple is in a small group of other disciples. Do everything you can to not just attend a small group but to get to know others in the group. Be there for them, serve them, encourage them, challenge them, pray for them and give to them.

Having done this, why not consider starting a small group and providing this environment for others?

Commit to helping new believers in their discipleship journey

While church leaders will do everything they can to help new converts grow and be established, what the new believer needs more than anything is a friend on the journey.

Take time to befriend and encourage the new believers you meet - ideally not with the opposite sex. Here are some practical things you can do:

- Be their friend.
- Sit with them in the church gathering.
- Invite them to your small group.
- Make sure they have a Bible and show them how to start reading it.
- Pray for them and offer to pray with them.
- Encourage them to be baptised.

Commit to the mission of Jesus

Disciples are to engage people with the gospel. Unless you are an evangelist you may find this one of the hardest things to do. Here are some tips:

- Deliberately have non-Christian friends.
- Pray for opportunities to share your faith.
- Pray for your friends to get saved.
- Tell God about your neighbours before you tell them about God.
- Look for every opportunity to practically demonstrate God's love and kindness to those who don't know Him.
- Be familiar with the gospel (see "The Romans Road" in Study 2).
- Never force your message down someone's throat. If you sense someone is resistant to what you're saying, then stop sharing. If you don't, they will avoid you in the future.
- Don't feel the pressure to tell them everything all at once. Just sow a seed and let God stir a hunger in them for more.
- If they ask you a hard question, it's ok to say: "I don't know the answer to that."

FREQUENTLY ASKED QUESTIONS

I HAVE SHARED THE GOSPEL SEVERAL TIMES WITH A FRIEND WHO CONTINUES TO BE DISINTERESTED IN GOD. WHAT SHOULD I DO?

The apostle Peter has advice for women who are married to husbands who do not believe:

> "Wives, in the same way submit yourselves to your own husbands so that, if any of them do not believe the word, they may be won over without words by the behaviour of their wives, when they see the purity and reverence of your lives." (1 Peter 3:1-2, NIV)

From what Peter says it is clear that the husband has heard the gospel but has chosen not to believe it. Instead of preaching to him over and over again (also known as nagging), Peter advises that the wife should preach through her actions. She is to move from declaring to demonstrating the love of God, from the words of the gospel to the works of the gospel.

While Peter was giving his advice to women with unbelieving husbands, it is clear this wise principle will also work with unbelieving wives, unbelieving friends or unbelieving work colleagues. Share the gospel, then show them the gospel.

Here are three simple things we can all do to effectively share the gospel with those around us: **pray, care, and share.**

It is good to **pray** for people who do not yet have a relationship with God. D.L. Moody, the famous 19th Century evangelist, prayed daily for 100 of his friends to come to know Christ. During his life, 96 of those friends gave their lives to Christ and at his funeral the final four joined them. While few of us could pray for that many people every day, the principle is important. Let's pray for those people in our lives who do not yet know God. Tell God about your neighbours before you tell your neighbours about God.

> "I urge, then, first of all, that petitions, prayers, intercession and thanksgiving be made for all people ... This is good, and pleases God our Saviour, who wants all people to be saved and to come to a knowledge of the truth." (1 Timothy 2:1, 3-4, NIV)

Another good prayer is to ask God to give you opportunities to share the gospel with people.

> "Pray for us, too, that God will give us many opportunities to speak ..." (Colossians 4:3, NLT)

One piece of research found that people have to hear the gospel on average seven times before they finally decide to follow Jesus. We must be patient and keep praying.

Having prayed, we must follow Peter's advice and **care** for people, thus demonstrating God's love. People don't care how much you know until they know how much you care. Constantly look for opportunities to serve and love people.

> "Let us not become weary in doing good, for at the proper time we will reap a harvest if we do not give up. Therefore, as we have opportunity, let us do good to all people ..." (Galatians 6:9-10, NIV)

Evangelism is like farming. The seed is the message about Jesus and the soil is the hearts of people. For the seed to go deep and grow, the ground first needs to be opened up - farmers call this ploughing the soil. God will use our prayers and our practical caring for people to open people's hearts to the message of Jesus.

As we pray and care for those around us, God will give us opportunities to **share**. There are two things we should share. Firstly, we can share our testimony, our story of how God has saved us. Secondly, we are to share the good news message about Jesus, which is called the gospel. Paul said, "… the gospel … is the power of God for salvation to everyone who believes …" (Romans 1:16, NASB). The message about Jesus's death and resurrection to save us from our sins has supernatural power - it is the most powerful seed we have.

There are two extremes Christians go to. Some are secret believers keeping their faith to themselves, never sharing the gospel. Others go to the other extreme and impose their message on others in a way that can make non-believers recoil. Let's instead make it our aim to lovingly and sensitively make the most of every opportunity to share our faith. Peter encourages us:

> "Always be prepared to give an answer to everyone who asks you to give the reason for the hope that you have. But do this with gentleness and respect …" (1 Peter 3:15-16, NIV)

LET'S BUILD TOGETHER

Nehemiah shared his vision and convictions with the people of God in his generation. In response, they declared: "Let's arise and build." (Nehemiah 2:18, NASB). They united around a conviction and went on to make history.

In every generation, God calls His people to build with conviction on the solid and unchanging foundation of His word, the Bible. Those who build this way are not only able to better withstand the storms of life (see Matthew 7:24-27) but are also empowered by God to change society.

Go Global is a growing family of churches with a vision to establish healthy, Bible-based and Spirit-empowered churches around the world. This series of seven studies, called Foundations, sums up our shared theological convictions - truths which both unify and define us as churches.

Foundations is our church membership course in Go Global churches. Having completed the seven studies, we now invite you to join us as we arise and build in our generation.

WHAT IS CHURCH MEMBERSHIP?

The moment you trust in Jesus as Saviour and Lord, the Holy Spirit supernaturally adds you to His great worldwide movement called the Church.

> "For by one Spirit we were all baptised into one body ..." (1 Corinthians 12:13, NASB)

Every believer is part of the worldwide church. However, it is vitally important for every believer to also be actively part of a local expression of the church where they live. We call this 'church membership'. The Bible is clear on what church membership involves:

- Church membership means you are committed to regularly gathering with the church and building meaningful relationships with other believers:

> "... not forsaking our meeting together as believers for worship and instruction, as is the habit of some, but encouraging one another; and all the more faithfully as you see the day of Christ's return approaching." (Hebrews 10:25, AMP)

- Church membership means you are willing to come under the care and oversight of a local church leadership team:

> "Obey your leaders and submit to them — for they keep watch over your souls as those who will give an account ..." (Hebrews 13:17, NASB)

> (See also 1 Thessalonians 5:12-13, Acts 20:28)

- Church membership means you are committed to playing your part in loving and serving others in the church community:

> "From him the whole body, joined and held together by every supporting ligament, grows and builds itself up in love, as each part does its work." (Ephesians 4:16, NIV)

"Therefore, as we have opportunity, let us do good to all people, especially to those who belong to the family of believers." (Galatians 6:10, NIV)

- Church membership means you are committed to generously supporting the church community with your financial giving:

"Remember this: Whoever sows sparingly will also reap sparingly, and whoever sows generously will also reap generously. Each of you should give what you have decided in your heart to give, not reluctantly or under compulsion, for God loves a cheerful giver. And God is able to bless you abundantly, so that in all things at all times, having all that you need, you will abound in every good work." (2 Corinthians 9:6-8, NIV)

- Church membership means you are consistently praying for your leaders and others in the church:

"… be alert and always keep on praying for all the Lord's people." (Ephesians 6:18, NIV)

WHAT ARE THE BENEFITS OF CHURCH MEMBERSHIP?

There are many benefits to being committed to a local church. Here are three of them:

- Firstly, as you are "planted in the house of the Lord", according to David, you can expect to flourish, grow strong and be fruitful for the long term (see Psalm 92:12-15).
- Secondly, as the committed core of a church grows, it is strengthened and empowered to see God's Kingdom come in its locality (see Acts 2:42-47).
- Thirdly, church leaders are accountable before God for how they lead and care for God's people (see Acts 20:28). It is therefore very important that the leaders know exactly who they are responsible for. A leader is not responsible for every person who visits the church, but they are responsible for every committed

member. At the point when they become members, the church leadership assumes responsibility for their spiritual care and growth.

ARE YOU READY FOR CHURCH MEMBERSHIP?

Here are three questions to honestly answer:

Are you saved and baptised in water?

In Study 2, 'The gospel and our response', we outlined what this means.

Do you agree with the truths we have studied?

Take a moment to reflect on the studies.

Are the truths we looked at your convictions?

Are you committed to building your life on these truths?

Agreeing with the same series of truths and having the same theological foundations enables the members of a church to be united. Truth becomes the basis for our unity.

Are you ready to be a committed church member?

As we have outlined above, being committed to a church is being committed to a local leadership and a community of believers. It involves investing your time, your love, your finances and your prayers. There is no perfect church, but God calls us to love and commit to the church just as He does.

If the answer to these three questions is a definite 'yes', then we are delighted to welcome you into membership.

WELCOME TO CHURCH MEMBERSHIP

As a follower of Jesus, I believe God calls me to live out my faith as a committed member of a local church. After prayerful consideration, I am committing to be a church member here at:

_____

[Church name]

_____

[Sign & date]

_____

[Church leader, sign & date]

ACKNOWLEDGEMENTS

In writing Foundations, I am deeply grateful for so many who have influenced and inspired me through their teachings, writings and example.

The greatest teacher of all is the Holy Spirit and the greatest source of wisdom is the Bible. Since becoming a follower of Jesus, at age 15, He has been my primary source of teaching. I distinctly remember moments reading scripture when the penny would drop and I would see a truth or a principle for the first time. These revelations have fuelled me and inspired my teachings through the years. I aspire to be a lifelong learner, being open to the Spirit's illumination and hungering for truth found in His word.

I and the rest of the world have been blessed by the courage and writing of Athanasius from the 4th Century whose legacy has been to articulate a clear understanding of the divinity of Jesus and the nature of God. C. S. Lewis, in more recent times, has greatly helped us grapple with the subject of God.

Nick Page, Amy Orr-Ewing and Vishal Mangalwadi have all produced excellent works looking at the Bible, its trustworthiness and its power to change the world. George Alexander's Old and New Testament overview and his lectures on Hermeneutics have proved very helpful.

I am thankful for the late Ern Baxter, whose teaching on baptism, leadership, the church, the Kingdom and the purpose of God gripped me as a young believer in the 1990s. God used him to paint an indelible vision on the canvas of my soul, a vision that has shaped my life, ministry and writing.

Terry Virgo, Charles Simpson, David Devenish and Bryn Jones have added so much to my understanding of the nature of the local church and church leadership. Indeed, Alan Scotland, Terry Virgo and David Holden have gone one step further and modelled their teaching with their humble, servant-hearted and fatherly leadership towards me.

Steve Murrell's writing and teaching on the subject of discipleship is first class and is rooted in years of effective ministry in Manila.

I am indebted to the leaders who have served alongside me over the years in the church in Edinburgh. From my earliest leadership team in the late 1990s until now, I have had the privilege of working alongside a great variety of gifted men and women. They continually model not only leadership gifting but also good character and godly wisdom. I am continually learning from them and count it an honour to have them in my life.

The church that Angie and I planted in 1998 has been my greatest classroom. Pastoring the congregation, planting new communities, raising leaders and preaching most weeks has changed me more than anything else. It continues to be a great honour for me and I consider it a stewardship from God.

Edd McCracken, who has been part of our church since the early days, is a good friend and an excellent journalist. I am grateful for his time and skill in editing this book.

In recent years, it has been the honour of my life to work with a growing international family of churches, many of which we planted from Edinburgh. I consider it a privilege to serve alongside courageous apostles, prophets, evangelists, pastors and teachers who are establishing churches, often in adverse situations. They are living lives completely devoted to God's church; many are serving the poor despite living in poverty themselves, and some live with threat as they preach the good news in hostile countries. All of them display huge measures of perseverance and faith. I am enriched by their lives and look forward to learning and growing with them in the years ahead.

To each intercessor who consistently prays for me and my family, I am deeply indebted for your love and service. Specifically, I want to express my heartfelt thanks to my fellow elder, Emperor Hatse, and my true brother, apostle Solomon S. Kalaga.

Finally, my wife Angie has been God's gift of wisdom to me. We are so different, and that's good. Her observations, timely challenge, gift of discernment and empathy for people have helped me with my many blind spots. We were married and started the church in the same month when we were both in our early twenties. She has served by my side all these years, despite many challenges and painful ministry experiences. Thank you, Angie, and thank you, God, for Angie.

"An excellent wife who can find? She is far more precious than jewels. The heart of her husband trusts in her, and he will have no lack of gain. She does him good, and not harm, all the days of her life." (Proverbs 31:10-12, ESV)